is also a universal story, beautifully written and passionately told, of a seeker on a dangerous journey, about the power of love and the eventual redemption that a child and family can bring. *Breakup* captures this in all its pain, joy, sadness, and mystery." —JANINE DI GIOVANNI, author of *Ghosts by Daylight: Love, War, and Redemption*

Bad News: Last Journalists in a Dictatorship

A Finalist for the PEN/John Kenneth Galbraith Award for Nonfiction • Winner of the Moore Prize • Amazon Book of the Year

"This . . . evocative account, focusing on young journalists struggling to gain the rights they so richly deserve, provides insights about the human condition that reach far beyond the tragic story of Rwanda." —NOAM CHOMSKY

"Anjan Sundaram is a keen observer and a fine writer. In *Bad News*, he has rendered a chilling chronicle of the creeping totalitarianism taking hold in Rwanda that is as disturbing as it is unforgettable." —JON LEE ANDERSON, author of *Che Guevara*

"Courageous and heartfelt." —*The Washington Post*

"A searing illustration of the dangers associated with news-gathering in an authoritarian state, and a paean to those courageous enough to practice it in such dire circumstances."
—*San Francisco Chronicle*

"It is nothing less than the best book written about Rwanda by an outsider, a massively important contribution to understanding what is one of Africa's most important, inscrutable regimes." —RICHARD POPLAK, *AllAfrica*

"A chilling account of reporters in danger that heightens awareness of the importance of a free press."
—*Kirkus Reviews*

"An important book for students of political science, modern history, and journalism." —*Publishers Weekly*

"Superb." —KENNETH ROTH, former executive director of Human Rights Watch

Stringer: A Reporter's Journey in the Congo

Book of the Year, The Royal African Society (UK)

"A remarkable book about the lives of people in Congo."
—JON STEWART, *The Daily Show*

"This is a book about a young journalist's coming of age, and a wonderful book it is, too." —TED KOPPEL, NPR

"An excellent debut book of reportage on the Congo." —FAREED ZAKARIA, CNN

"Anjan Sundaram's prose is so luscious, whether he's writing about mathematics or colonial architecture or getting mugged, that the words come alive and practically dance on the page. *Stringer*, his first book, is about a yearlong journey to Congo; reading it made me feel like I'd follow him anywhere in the world." —BARBARA DEMICK, author of *Nothing to Envy: Ordinary Lives in North Korea* and *Logavina Street: Life and Death in a Sarajevo Neighborhood*

"What a debut! It's not often one reads a book of reportage from a difficult foreign country with such fever-dream immediacy, such tense intelligence, and such an artful gift for storytelling. Here is a commanding new writer who comes to us with the honesty, the intensity, and the discerning curiosity of the young Naipaul." —PICO IYER, author of *The Lady and the Monk*, *The Global Soul*, and *The Man Within My Head*

"In lucid and searing prose, and with bracing self-awareness, Anjan Sundaram explores a country that has long been victimized by the ever-renewed greeds of the modern world.

Stringer is one of those very rare books of journalism that transcend their genre—and destiny as ephemera—and become literature." —PANKAJ MISHRA, author of *From the Ruins of Empire* and *Temptations of the West*

"With an incisive intellect and senses peeled raw, Sundaram takes us on a mesmerizing journey through the vibrant shambles of modern Congo. This is that rare work of reportage that achieves true literary greatness, and it can stand proudly next to V. S. Naipaul or Ryszard Kapuściński." —RICHARD GRANT, author of *God's Middle Finger*

BREAKUP

ALSO BY ANJAN SUNDARAM

Bad News: Last Journalists in a Dictatorship

Stringer: A Reporter's Journey in the Congo

BREAKUP

A MARRIAGE
IN WARTIME

ANJAN SUNDARAM

CATAPULT  NEW YORK

First Catapult edition: 2023

ISBN: 978-1-64622-115-8

Library of Congress Control Number: 2022947251

Jacket design and illustration by Jaya Miceli
Book design by tracy danes

Catapult
New York, NY
books.catapult.co

Printed in the United States of America

10 9 8 7 6 5 4 3 2 1

To journalists everywhere
whose work has cost them,
to my family

CONTENTS

BREAKUP

Home, in Canada

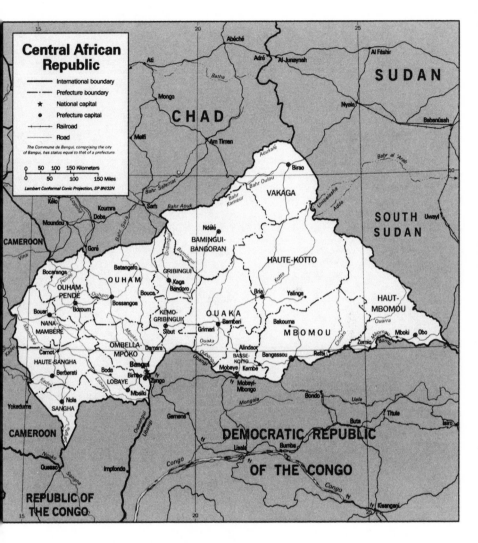

The Central African Republic, circa 2013

FAMILY

I MOVED AWAY FROM THE WORLD, AND MY FAMILY gave me refuge. In my wife's embrace, in the bliss of my home, I believed I could never again be alone, never again be helpless.

In July 2013, I became a father. Raphaëlle's birth reinforced our family. She looked fragile, so obviously mortal. She brought me new obligations, as a father: to work and earn money.

But she did far more. I looked down over her, and lifted her up in my arms, and thought she could not be all that I left behind, of myself, in the world. My work acquired a new significance. It became a way to nourish and shelter her, and also to take distance from her. I searched my past, seeking work to which I felt an old connection, that had shaped me, and to which my link felt elemental, pure, necessary.

The most isolated major war in the world was then underway, in a country called the Central African Republic, among the world's most sparsely populated places. This conflict was perhaps even more deadly than the Syrian war, which at the time dominated newspaper headlines. But Central Africa, home to several long-running wars, rarely made the first page.

I had learned journalism a decade before, just south of the Central African Republic. My first job out of college was in the Democratic Republic of the Congo, as a "stringer"—a freelance journalist paid ten U.S. cents per published word—for the U.S. wire agency the Associated Press. I learned a great deal more from Rwandan reporters whom I taught as their government imprisoned them and even killed some of our colleagues.

The obscurity of this new Central African war made it difficult to justify a trip to report on it. I needed to consider the costs: for the flight and travel, and of journeying through an isolated terrain, far from my family.

My wife, Nat, and I were then in a fusional marriage. She had also worked as a war correspondent. We had met in the Democratic Republic of the Congo, where she had managed a United Nations radio station on the war's northeastern front line.

Nat had helped me break some of my early war stories. From the front she sent me intelligence about deadly attacks; I typed them up and e-mailed them to the Associated Press right as her radio station broadcast the story. Speed was paramount to a wire reporter, and Nat helped me, a rookie in Congo, outpace my competition.

I had turned down a job on Wall Street to try to become a journalist in Congo, and those first published stories gave me the courage to stay there and cover the war. The initial trust between Nat and me bloomed into love, and then marriage. Now we planned on growing old together, and our desire for a permanent attachment had led us to birth our wailing infant.

I found it difficult to persuade magazine editors to commission a story. "Which central African republic?" they asked. The alternative was to finance the journey myself, and hope that any payments I later received—from one of these editors—covered my costs.

The war's obscurity was galling. Not only for its great tumult, or for its many unrecorded killings, but for its historical importance. This war marked a reversal of colonial history in Central Africa. The rebels who had taken over the country were mostly Muslim. And their victory marked the first Muslim rule here since powerful Muslim kingdoms were defeated by French armies in the late nineteenth century. Almost a hundred years after the French established their brutal African colonies, Muslims still remembered their ancestors' humiliation, and sought to recover glory.

There was now talk of a religious conflict in the Central African Republic, of Christians rising up to fight their new Muslim rulers, of old grievances resurfacing, of an implicit and long-unchallenged Christian dominance at stake. The winner ruled a land rich with gold, diamonds, and the ivory of forest elephants.

And in part because it happened in Central Africa, in part because this region and nearby Congo had been rife with war, in part because we easily dismiss violence as savagery, unworthy of our attention, this great war passed in relative obscurity.

I felt isolated by knowing anything at all about the Central African Republic. The events I investigated—a coup d'état, killings, a rebellion—were historic, yet almost no one around me had heard of them. This magnified my sense of isolation.

To care about things that seemed irrelevant to the society around me produced a dislocation. But secure at home, embraced by love, I persisted with my research.

Family's loyalty and intimacy, and the paternal labors of Raphaëlle's diaper replacements and constant feedings, newly grounded me. My domestic routines became an anchor from which to engage one of the most isolated parts of our world.

In my office, my wooden desk was a mess as I researched a country I had never before looked at this closely. On loose pages I summarized articles, conversations with university researchers, and ideas about things to investigate; I plotted a route through the war's deadliest sites.

My office was dark, and its old desk, which had belonged to Nat's father, was lit by a single lamp; the room's only brightness was its fluorescent orange carpet. I worked, surrounded by a quiet in the house, and seemingly for miles around me, in our coastal town.

A researcher I spoke with delivered disturbing news. I had to speed up my preparations: the new Muslim government in the Central African Republic had announced it would block roads leading in and out of the capital. This would further isolate the war.

Information about the violence was already scarce. Soldiers had destroyed radio station antennae and attacked local journalists. People feared speaking out, even when their families were assaulted. An entire village was destroyed, but an incomplete report had emerged only weeks later.

As the war thrashed across the country, its front line concealed, Central African people hardly knew what happened to one another, even a few kilometers from their homes. So nearly blind, like everyone, I planned to start in the capital, Bangui, and drive toward that destroyed village.

It was how I stabbed ahead.

At the time, I lived with Nat and Raphaëlle on Canada's Atlantic coast. Our town was called Shippagan, which meant "passage of the ducks." Fewer than a thousand families lived in the town, and everyone knew Nat's father had run the local school, and that her mother had worked at the post office. This close-knit and safe community was perfect for new parents, though its poverty made it unlikely we could stay indefinitely. Shippagan was a fishing town, and where its lobster and crab had once made it rich, it depended on government handouts now that the ocean was depleted. A university campus and marine laboratory were important employers, and a provincial aquarium attracted regional tourists.

Late that morning, having worked into the night, I set aside my notes on the Central African Republic, and carried Raphaëlle to the aquarium to visit its blue crabs. We found the crabs in their shallow tank, beside pebbles and seashells. Raphaëlle reached out, her fingers outstretched to touch the blue shells. A sign on the wall said it was forbidden. But I leaned forward to bring her close. The crabs didn't move. They looked sick. Perhaps they should never have been removed from the ocean. The aquarium seemed a sad edifice, housing dying marine life. We looked at coral and large fish in their glass cases, and watched a baby seal thrust madly across its little pool, as if doing laps. Raphaëlle, observing the seal's metronomic delirium, leaned against my chest. I looked down, and she fell asleep. I left the aquarium, walking home along the beach, feeling her breaths blow up my neck. The shore was covered in pebbles. I wondered if these pebbles had all washed in with the tide. Then they moved, dozens at once, slowly. They were snails.

Shippagan's fishing season was over, so these beaches were hardly frequented. Brightly painted boats sat on stilts in parking lots. The sea shimmered. We turned a corner onto *rue Bellefeuille*, the "street of beautiful leaves." Our lawn gleamed in the twilight. Behind the trees stood our single-story house, typical for this region, made of horizontal white slats. Nat's father had built it about forty years before, right across from the local school. Our neighbors included a hairdresser, a carpenter, and a psychiatrist.

Raphaëlle's sweet breath blew into my nostrils. I lay her down in her rocker, in my bedroom. Then I descended the creaking stairs to my desk in the basement, my other world. I expected a call from a companion who would make my journey less desolate, who had the budget to rent a car. Lewis was from upper-class Boston and lived in Rwanda, where we had worked together. He was an investigator for the nonprofit Human Rights Watch. I'd spent many late nights at his Kigali house, drinking fine whisky, discussing Rwanda's secret torture program and dissidents' disappearances.

We also shared a complicity from working on the bottom rungs of corporate America: he on Wall Street, at Macquarie Bank; and I in San Francisco, at McKinsey & Company. He still wore bright bankers' socks. We were brusque with each other, and it showed our trust: when my sister visited Rwanda, he'd asked, "Can I seduce her? Or will you punch me in the face?" Later, I'd turned to him when the Rwandan government pursued me.

On the phone, we debated how to drive into the war. Satellites would help. Lewis told me Human Rights Watch had received satellite photos of an attack in the Central African Republic. We stared at two sets of images: one from a few weeks before and the other just days old. The photographs showed villages—clusters of houses. The houses were neat squares; and in the older images the squares' thatch roofs shone, reflecting the sun. In the recent photos, those same squares were dark. The thatch roofs had been burned off, and we looked into the houses' bleak interiors.

We plotted each photograph's coordinates as points to investigate.

We needed to obtain our visas at a French embassy—the Central African Republic's former colonial master was still responsible for much of the country's foreign affairs. We had partied a few months before with the French consul in Kigali. Lewis suggested it would be easiest to process my visa through him.

I hung up, and the house regained its silence. I heard footsteps above: Nat's familiar walk. I waited for the sounds, which brought me warmth and comfort while I worked in the basement.

I spread my travel gear on the orange carpet. I had to pack for hot and cool weather, and not too heavy, so we could move fast. Medication was important: for malaria, other fevers, disinfecting wounds, and ordinary stomach ailments, any of which could become critical if we were far from a clinic. I carried pills to purify water. A tent? A waterproof jacket? How many shoes? I had laid out too many things. I squatted and sorted through them.

We prepared for a diversity of terrains, some of the world's richest in rare plants and wildlife, and also some of its most beautiful. In the country's south were rainforests and elephant sanctuaries in the great Congo Basin. The northern deserts extended to Chad, Sudan, and the Sahel. Between the forest and desert lay savanna.

I imagined our journey: by car, on foot in places, and by motorcycle. We would sleep in villages. I added rubber slippers to my pile, a spare pair of spectacles, and antihistamines for my dust allergies.

Already my backpack was full. This was all I would carry. Writing was a simple profession; I had chosen it, in part, for its simplicity, which allowed me independence. I needed less money and equipment than a radio or television reporter; I was less beholden to the caprices of financiers.

Traveling lighter, and less obtrusively, it was easier for me to get into places. I won people's confidence as I watched, and recorded; I corroborated others' experiences.

For years I had heard about this country. I knew of the infamous Lord's Resistance Army, a rebellion that sought shelter in Central African forests as U.S. soldiers hunted it down. A faction in Congo's war had sent fighters into Bangui: its leader, Jean-Pierre Bemba, was later convicted in The Hague for war crimes committed by these troops. The Central African Republic made the news when power shifted and, even then, hardly. From the outside, it could seem like an oblivion, a country in the high seas. The closest I had gotten to it was while reporting from Congo's rainforest, when I had peered in over its border.

In Lewis I had a good companion. We cared for each other. Alone, I worried I might make a rash decision, be blind to a risk, or lose my bearings.

Lewis documented massacres in the Central African Republic for Human Rights Watch. He assigned responsibility for them, collecting evidence to a legal standard, so lawyers could convict the perpetrators in international human rights courts. I complemented his work, documenting people's experiences. Recording the emotions of the war, I conveyed it to others. I was permitted, outside of a strict moral or judicial framework, to follow the perpetrators' logic. I tracked people who fled the war and those who fought back against their violators. Together, Lewis and I documented the war's past and present, gathering testimony of people's courage.

I looked up flights online, scrolling through the options. That night, I lay face up with my arms by my sides. I considered all the things I had packed, wondering what I had missed. I wrestled with the scenes that my mind threw up from an imaginary war—all false, but that felt real. After a two-hour struggle, I went to Nat's room and snuggled up against her. She put her arm around me. And when she had dissolved my anxiety I returned to my bed, near Raphaëlle's rocker.

The isolation and obscurity of that other world—I felt I had already entered a cave, and found myself alone inside. Around me, the community, family, and the child's clamor were distant.

When I noticed the child, quickly the events I read about died away to a whisper; my mind forgot them. The clamor, so proximate and blatant, reminded me how easily our world's great noises, cries, and explosions are drowned.

Then the Central African Republic faded, leaving no trace, no whiff to follow, nothing of it to hold on to—and I was a father, embroiled in the immediate, the loud, the fear of my child falling, or falling sick, of her mortality, and also mine.

I woke up late, again, the next day, and was in a hurry to check the news, in case the government had announced another blockade. Nat laughed at how quickly I went from my bed to the bathroom to my desk. I had half departed from Canada, and our family; Nat chided me that Raphaëlle was ready for feeding.

My bed stayed unmade until the afternoon, when I grew tired of work. I made my bed so it promised relief, invited me to rest. I should have rested more.

The days passed, and we approached my flight. I took on more of the house's chores, knowing that once I left Nat would be burdened by the need to constantly sweep up dust, put clothes to wash, hang them up, fold them. Doing the chores felt like a charade, a way to diminish the pain of my departure.

The clothes bin filled up in a day, and the dust returned in two; hair from our bodies and heads fell on the white bathroom floor. All things remained at a point of stasis, a meaningless calm. I felt the need to get out, go somewhere with our family. I did not drive, so I asked Nat if she would take us to the coast.

She drove us to Miscou Island Lighthouse. I looked out over the waters; the sea was dark. You could see the Gaspé

Peninsula, named after the Mi'kmaq word *gespeg*, which meant "land's end." And indeed, it felt like the farthermost point on earth. The sky and sea dominated as a uniform gray. We had good visibility, and I thought I could see all the way north to the Arctic. Nat stood on high ground, photographing the majestic landscape and me walking on the beach.

Nat showed me her pictures. I looked pensive, staring at my feet on the immense beach. I missed our house's warmth. We drove past a bingo club, where the elderly played. The towns here were full of pensioners, and so they were quiet. Acadia's youth had fled the economic crisis. Many of them manned heavy machinery in Alberta's oil sands. The towns were abandoned.

Nat asked if Lewis and I had planned our route, if we knew our first stop. I told her we had a possible lead southwest from Bangui. And the burned-up towns were in the country's far west. "We're just guessing," I said. "We have to go there."

My words did not reassure. I knew my journey would become more difficult the farther I traveled. But I had control over my route and how I navigated the chaos. Nat would wait, knowing less and less, hoping I had good luck. I tried to let Nat shape my journey. She searched for contacts in the Central African Republic who could help me if I ran into trouble. Lewis had arranged to bring a satellite phone so she and I could be in touch from even the most remote areas.

We drove past *l'île Lamèque* (Lamèque Island), the

subject of a local joke because the remote island sounded like *La Mecque*, French for "Mecca," the center of the Muslim world. Most people here hadn't traveled outside their province, New Brunswick. *La Baie des Chaleurs*, the "Bay of Warmth," appeared on our right. Tranquil, glistening like a lake. Nat asked if I felt prepared. Her fingers shifted over the steering wheel. "Preparation is most important," she said, "you can't be taking decisions in the heat of it."

I looked across at her, not wanting to consider her cautionary words. I looked at her hair, which had turned a lighter hue that summer, from the sun. And I wondered from where the tension arose—if from her stasis. She breastfed and could not come with me.

"Bangui, Bangui, Bangui," she said, repeating the word in different tones to make a music. "You'll call me." She had found only a few books about the Central African Republic, mostly aimed at academics. "It's as if this country doesn't exist for the average reader. No wonder so few people know about this war."

"Why is that, do you think?"

"It feels so far away, *tellement loin*," she said, "my man, you come home safe."

Then she cackle-laughed. "I've made you nervous," she said.

She spoke about a book called *Femmes de Dictateur*, or Dictator's Wives, a feminist retelling that restored the centrality of dictators' wives who'd been erased from history.

She told me about the former Central African president Jean-Bédel Bokassa, who had proclaimed himself emperor, and thus the Central African Republic an empire. His wife and France had fed his delusions, organizing a coronation like Napoleon's, with white horses and antique Napoleonic swords provided by Saint-Cyr, the French military college in Paris. Bokassa had been toppled after murdering nearly a hundred children in Bangui. He then anointed himself the thirteenth apostle of Jesus. He had died in 1996.

I felt the anxiety in her idle chatter. I settled firm in my seat, wary that an explosion might follow.

She asked for a gift. She wanted something pretty. The Central African Republic was known for sculptors who carved ebony necklaces and engraved calabashes. I'd heard of its famous tableaux, collages of tropical butterfly wings. I might buy her a recording of polyphonic *ngombi* melodies, or modern rumba—close to the Congolese music we listened to at home. "If I can get them past Canadian customs," I said, "I'll bring Raphaëlle some *chenilles*." White stubby caterpillars, sold live in markets, prized for their protein and known as "Central African caviar." Nat grinned, her hands steadier. She had rolled her sleeves up to her elbows. The bay rose beside us to the level of the road, as if its waters might be perturbed and flood beneath us.

Nat accelerated. We passed grassy plains, manicured gardens, and a Catholic church on a cliff slope that angled toward the ocean.

On my last two days at home I rooted myself in

Raphaëlle's routine. I bathed and fed her and walked with her on the beach. Her ears lay against my chest, where my heart beat. My house chores produced a feeling of order.

On the last afternoon I sat in an old rocking chair reading an analyst report about the origins of the new Central African government, and about Bangui, our first port of call.

Raphaëlle and I invented a game that gave her a sense of her own strength. She kicked my face and I crashed into the wall; delighted, she gurgled. Nat interrupted us suddenly, entered our room. She had dug up the name of a Bangui journalist—she handed me a slip with his contact information. It was the research she had mentioned in the car; that tension had culminated, and was gone. Each preparation brought home the journey's risk. She just stood there. I got up and embraced her.

She had penetrated into my isolation. The Central African journalist, Thierry, was our home's ambassador in a remote outpost. I was already safer. She said Thierry was available for our assignment and willing to meet in Bangui to hear more about our mission. Most important, before we traveled together, we needed to test if we got along.

That midnight, in the basement, I read about Inuit seal hunts. The book had belonged—along with most of our library, mounted on the basement's wall—to Nat's father. He had died of a heart attack before I met Nat. I read the

book as a way of invoking someone older, wiser, an ances-
tor. I preferred to spend such moments of acute fear in the
company of the dead, in reading the classics or listening to
old music. I turned down the lights and played his Johnny
Cash vinyl on the gramophone. I danced by myself, flailing
my limbs.

I felt haunted by Acadia's bright skies, and by the joy
of birth. My relationship with Raphaëlle was nascent. And
it was a time of a kind of annihilation in me—suddenly, I
felt double in the world, and at the same time, as if a part
of me had been consumed, that I had given up myself. Her
eyes were expressive. I felt her birth brought my death into
the world; she raised the question of what I left behind
when I was gone. So I felt a thrill at her presence along
with a void—the sense of death as well as the opening to
immortality. This paradoxical experience of procreation was
charged, euphoric, troubling.

Nat saw me off at the door when my taxi arrived. I left
while Raphaëlle was still asleep in her crib. And in that last
moment, when I stepped out, I felt overcome; I was now
a father who left his family and went to work, who was
absent.

There was no stepping back in.

The flights became portals: they opened in one place,
hundreds of kilometers away. People in the airports looked
lost despite holding their tickets. I floated between them,
disconnected, and too tired to begin conversations, I moved
in a daze. We flew in a great spiral. Kigali was only a

thousand kilometers from Bangui. But only two airlines operated the last leg, into the war, so Lewis and I had to fly more than three thousand kilometers from Rwanda, first to Ethiopia and then Cameroon.

Confused by my departure, I told myself I should be relieved that the child's clamor, the numbing household chores, and the stifling comfort and security of my home were behind me. But I wasn't convinced. The joy of my closeness to Raphaëlle became strained. The road forced me to look ahead, leading away from my anchor, but offering the potential of connection with strangers. I needed home, and wanted it, but gladly departed from it. And I realized that I had built my home because I was afraid, as a place in which to hide when I feared the world's capriciousness.

On our half-day stopover in Cameroon, Lewis and I lunched on the Atlantic coast, under a thatch roof, the seabirds flying low over us. The chef grilled us a fish fresh from a bucket of seawater. A fellow diner shouted that his wallet had been stolen while he'd been in the toilet. He shouted too much; Lewis and I inspected the toilet. Inside, a giant rat stared at us. "You used this toilet with this giant rat here?" Lewis said. The diner said the rat had eaten his wallet.

On our third flight, I stared through the cabin windows at the clouds. For a moment, I felt the panic of having no responsibilities. I imagined Nat watching the TV news as she fed Raphaëlle. My thoughts, just now rushing, turned quiet.

Our aircraft circled Bangui in the night. The capital was shaped as a triangle, and the wide Ubangi River, beside it, was a black expanse. Yellow points shone on its riverbanks—homes. Out from the capital, into the countryside, stretched a black continuum. I stepped out of the aircraft to the engine's high and low hums. Our flight was the only arrival that night. As I walked to the low airport terminal, silence enveloped us, and I heard my footsteps.

Soldiers in the customs hall emptied and searched my knapsack, marking it as safe with a white X using chalk. I waited outside for Lewis. His bags took longer to inspect: besides the satellite phone, he had brought his computer. We each carried our professional digital cameras, to take pictures of the war crime scenes.

I smelled a burning and surveyed the horizon. The parking lot glistened under the airport lights. We drove down the Avenue des Martyrs, which, without warning or signpost, suddenly expanded wide: this had been the colonial airport runway. And we entered Bangui's *kodros*, village-like neighborhoods of mud houses and tin roofs. Sometimes, a black space appeared: this was a rural capital, a "city-garden," whose corn and manioc fields ran through public grounds and alongside its main roads. People sat outside on their porches; the electricity was cut. The country was bankrupt.

I arrived in this new place, off the long flights, feeling empty. I had lost myself, as if some part of my being had still not arrived here and was still in transit. I reached for my phone. Rwanda's networks did not roam here. We needed to buy local SIM cards.

Our guesthouse for the night, called the Relais des
Chasses (or the Hunting Lodge), shocked me out of my
dislocation. I stood before a building so bright it burned
my eyes. On the outside, it resembled a military base. Bulbs
lined the restaurant's ceiling. Liquor bottles glowed in the
bar. A generator at the back of the compound emitted a low
rumble, powering all these lights. The compound shone too
bright; I felt the city's neighborhoods watched us from the
dark, under our spotlight.

I preferred arriving with discretion, so I knew a place
as it was, and could diminish my foreignness. I tried to
strike up conversations with people in line at a food stall,
or buying telephone credit. This guesthouse was an em-
barrassment. We had arrived like dignitaries, authorities,
as people of power—like people who could display themselves ostentatiously and exclude themselves from the surrounding crisis. This guesthouse distrusted the city. Its
owner, Freddy, a former French soldier close to the Central African government, had likely paid off the local mafias to keep his clients safe. His protection was expensive:
Freddy charged us three hundred dollars per night, near
an average Central African's annual income. I was not of
his clientele, I thought. And all the burning lights, they
reactivated my isolation.

I grasped for a closeness to home. I sent Nat photos of
the guesthouse over its fast Internet. Nat called me, and said,
"You're sending me pictures of light bulbs, *des ampoules*."

"I feel watched. I don't like them."

My speech was tight.

"That's how soldiers defend," she said. "They build fortresses."

Lewis and I hired an old sedan, a yellow Nissan Sunny taxi that rolled and pitched, like an airplane, over Bangui's uneven roads. The driver said his seat belts had been stolen, so I clutched at the handle above my window as I jumped in my seat. The buildings made a low sprawl. Driving through the city was one way of piercing through our isolation.

We passed a woman wearing a short skirt, who turned and stared inside our taxicab, straight at us. We slowly overtook her. Lewis leaned into the backseat and looked up through the rear window.

I said, "Not feeling well?"

"Shit."

His waist was depressed, as if hollow, into the crack where our seat met the backrest.

He finally spoke: "I can't say this to many friends. My Casanova days are over."

Our homes risked blowing apart. The world, and its sensations, presented constant risks. Lewis had been a ladies' man. But less than a year after he had met his wife, already they were married, with a son. So we were both new fathers. And the provocation of that pedestrian's stare—its arousal—was limited to our imaginations.

I asked where we were headed.

"To meet a U.N. official," Lewis said, flipping through his notes.

We found an official who, instead of informing us, hoped that we could educate him. When I asked where we should travel, he read out the numbers of people displaced in an attack two months before. "I'm asking about now," I said. These officials were rarely allowed to leave the capital, because their agencies feared they might be abducted or ransomed; some aid workers here had been killed. The official said he didn't know what happened even twenty kilometers from where we sat.

I said, "Nobody knows?"

He threw up his hands. "We don't run any field missions. It's too dangerous outside Bangui."

So the capital was cut off. It could be attacked at any time, and would only know at the last minute. The officials meanwhile passed the time in their air-conditioned offices powered by generators.

The other aid worker we met, for lunch in an open-air restaurant, arrived sweating, wearing a helmet and bulletproof vest. His hand got caught in his helmet strap and he spilled food over his bulky vest. A shootout might start in the middle of the day. He said a cease-fire had been called in Bossangoa, a northern city, and suggested we go—about the rest of the country, he had little idea.

The capital was quiet. The radio mostly played Congolese rumba, lacking reports about the conflict. Our Nissan

Sunny slowly made its way through the city with a sticker on its dashboard that said TRANQUILITÉ.

We heard about the massacre, at a remote site in the jungle, that evening. It had allegedly been perpetrated two weeks before; to us, in Bangui, this was news.

We met Thierry—Nat's contact—back at our guesthouse, the *Relais des Chasses*.

He was a short, bald man. He wore a long-sleeve shirt, blue and with bright blue buttons, untucked over his jeans. His leather shoes were wrinkled, as if recently drenched. Our beer bottles glinted green on our table, under the lights. A European couple stood at the bar, the woman wearing a backless dress, looking extraordinarily vulnerable. Freddy came by to serve us peanuts, and I raised an eyebrow at the couple.

"They run the Heineken factory," Freddy said.

"Business is good now?" I said.

"Very."

Thierry leaned forward.

"You know of a massacre?" I said.

He told us there was a town called Gaga, about 250 kilometers west of Bangui, where soldiers had slaughtered over a hundred people.

"Has it been reported already?" I said. "How come we never heard of it?"

He said the journalists didn't dare broadcast the news. The government denied that its soldiers committed crimes; journalists let the massacres pass unreported.

Thierry spoke without expression, without raising his voice.

"This is how the government controls the narrative," he said. "When no one speaks about the massacres, how will anyone know?"

If we believed the brief radio bulletins between long spells of rumba, we might think this country was largely at peace, but for the odd crime. We would believe that no villages had been burned. And that the soldiers protected the people.

This void of information was filled by a general paranoia about who might attack, when, from where, and how. Rumors spread about imminent attacks, or attacks that had just happened, all difficult to verify.

The war was fought between the government and rebels. The president, Michel Djotodia, was a political theorist and polyglot. He shaped the movement known as the Seleka ("the alliance") before it had seized power a few months before. The mostly Muslim Seleka conquered the capital. Its soldiers committed atrocities as they tried to hold on to the provinces.

When the Seleka's forces were accused of war crimes, Djotodia officially abolished the Seleka. Henceforth, international reports could not mention the group, which could thus no longer be responsible for crimes since it no longer existed. Central Africans were meanwhile attacked by their own government. The U.N. recognized Djotodia as the country's legitimate authority and negotiated with him, because he controlled the country's most powerful military force.

The violence was absurd.

The U.N. was not going to stop Djotodia. So ordinary people gathered their homemade weapons and formed a rebellion called the *anti-balaka* (or "the anti-bullets"). At first glance, the government was vastly more powerful. But if the rebels—mostly Christian, like roughly 80 percent of this country—could somehow win, they might kill the toppled Muslim officials and the country's 15 percent Muslim minority.

Meanwhile, the U.N., France, and the African Union had sent their soldiers—called international peacekeepers—to protect the president and his allies. The French flag flew atop Bangui's airport, a symbol that the country's former colonial power was here to "restore order."

"What do you think we should do?" I said.

"Dunno, man," Lewis replied, shaking his head.

"Go in?"

Lewis pulled up his leather belt, embossed with L.M.M., his initials, in brass. He looked at me, awaiting an answer, his breath heavier.

I asked Thierry if he was willing to take us to Gaga, the site of the alleged massacre. Lewis added he would hire him as a research assistant.

Thierry said he had wanted to report on the massacre, but lacked the funds for a car and fuel. It was why he pitched us the story. We made a good match. We discussed his terms of payment.

At last, Thierry's stern expression gave way to a smile. He said, "I have been waiting for a chance to reach Gaga."

He left to gather his belongings, giving Lewis and me each an *mporo*, a collegial handshake followed by a click of the fingers, a good sign. Nat's contact had proved crucial. And I felt she had approved of our journey to Gaga. I never told Thierry, but his presence had this greater significance: I felt a closeness to him, and a sense of security, like from home.

Our next task was to find transport. One of Lewis's colleagues had recommended a driver named Suleiman, who asked us to meet him near Bangui's central roundabout, at a pastry shop. We found him seated outside, his legs crossed as he ate the cream off a cupcake and licked his white-stained fingers.

"Ho!" he greeted us.

He stood, and we looked up: he towered over us.

"We talk?" Lewis said, and Suleiman nodded. "We'll show you where." Lewis searched in his bag. We ordered black coffee and croissants, unfolded a map of the country, and traced our fingers along the road to Gaga.

"That's okay," Suleiman said, "but where from there?" He pointed out many roads that had been blocked, and others that were too dangerous. He indicated off-map routes. "You'll have to trust me," he said. It was true: in many places we would have no cell phone network, and our compasses would be useless, because the Central African Republic lay over a "magnetic anomaly."

Suleiman's pickup truck was clean, spotless white. We all agreed to leave the next day. Lewis and I had done as well as we could have hoped: we had a destination and a team.

I was impatient to leave Bangui's isolation, its ignorance, its impotent waiting.

We paid Suleiman to buy fuel—it was a symbolic transaction, confirming we had hired him, that we would make this journey. In the evening, Suleiman drove Lewis and me to our new accommodations, at a small church that operated a guesthouse for humanitarian and religious travelers. Two church sisters received us. Two kittens rested in the church's courtyard.

I noticed we had stored our two-hundred-liter barrel of extra fuel—which Freddy had purchased for us—outside my room.

"Why *my* room?" I said to Lewis.

He claimed he had not noticed.

"It's a hazard. I'm not sleeping with this thing here."

And I was about to berate Lewis about the need for trust—that when we drove into the war I should not be left out of such decisions—when I realized we would carry our extra fuel with us, on our journey, aboard our truck. The government's fighters had destroyed most rural petrol stations as they had marched toward the capital. And so, sullenly, I helped tie the barrel to the back of Suleiman's pickup, behind our seats, where it sat like a bomb. A stray bullet or cigarette would be enough to ignite it.

These risks were unavoidable.

I checked in with the sisters and returned to the parking lot to find Suleiman sucking on a pipe, to draw fuel out of the barrel. When he felt the petrol touch his lips he thrust the pipe into the pickup's tank.

The fuel stopped flowing; Suleiman again sucked. I told him petrol was carcinogenic, and might kill him. But he laughed. He had used this technique since he was a boy. "I don't think a cancer will be what kills me." He cupped his hands over the tube and sucked, and we were engulfed by the sweet, intoxicating fumes. Suleiman now heaved, out of breath.

I asked the others to delay our departure. I felt we needed to pause. We had prepared too quickly, and I thought we departed too soon after our arrival in the country. Once we were outside Bangui we would need all our calm and our wits. So, better we rest one day, I thought.

Our brand-new team, still unfamiliar with one another, would in a few hours drive out to investigate Thierry's report of a massacre. We came together on that day, out of necessity or fear I could not be sure, and expressed our recklessness.

Suleiman drove us to a posh supermarket, its entrance crowded by beggars. None of them stepped inside or attempted to raid the market of its expensive foods. A wealthy Central African woman ambled through its aisles, picking out jars; otherwise it was empty. Tubelights lit up its bleach-colored tiles.

We ran our trolley through the aisles, pulling boxes of French chocolate off the shelves. We ate candy and cream puffs inside the store—we craved sweet. The biscuit aisle was a child's paradise—its pastries were topped with dark and milk chocolate and filled with fruit jams. We drugged ourselves on the sugar. We left the supermarket in a frenzy; outside, in the sun, I became exhausted, and ashamed. Our spree betrayed our lack of psychological preparedness. The anxiety overwhelmed us.

A man in a ragged jacket stepped up to me. I thought I had seen him at the entrance on my way in. He stared at the street. "*Ça va?*" I asked. "You're okay?" He said his wife had left him in the war, and he had walked to Bangui, over days, through ravaged towns. He recited their names: Ngoula, Mboum, Aya, Banza . . .

That evening, before we left Bangui, I sought out a government official—the government was, after all, responsible for most of the atrocities.

I met General Abdel Kader Kalil on his villa's porch, where he stood with his arms outstretched. "*As-salaam alai-kum*," I said. "Peace be unto you." He asked if I was Muslim; I explained that I had grown up in Dubai. He raised his eyebrows.

A tailor stepped up from behind him and measured his

lengths, holding one end of the tape in his armpits. On a large ironing table lay a drawing of a man's suit, and pieces of cloth marked in pink wax. When the measuring was done, the general seated himself on a wooden throne, and adjusted the ends of his *kaftan*, his traditional long shirt. "We will make this place into a second Dubai." So this was the government's dream: Dubai, that beacon of financial success, and relative peace, in the Islamic world.

"I will bring the technological age to Africa," he said. "Help me raise money."

He declared himself *un enfant du pays*, "a child of the country." During their coup d'état, enemy fighters were so afraid of him, he said, that they had scattered when he fired a single shot. He had defeated a well-trained South African company on his way into Bangui. During that battle he saw a pigeon flutter on the ground, before realizing it was twitching flesh that a bomb had ripped out of his own buttocks.

"Many Muslims died," I said.

"*Shuhada*," he whispered. Martyrs.

"But the general conquered this country," I said, referring to him in the third person as a sign of respect, "ensuring their deaths were not in vain."

The general became morose. His euphoria suddenly waned. We heard the tailor snip cloth, and sometimes the air, at his table. The general put his head in his hands and bent over. I placed my hand on the general's back to comfort him.

The general's aide-de-camp—so far silent—offered me *"précision,"* as he called it. For this new government to survive, it had to decisively win the war. The Christian rebels were driven by hate. The proof: they hid in the forests and avoided dialogue with the United Nations. And from their hideouts they created more and more violence.

"But everyone's blaming the government for the killings," I said.

"The Christians have killed us for a hundred years."

The general perhaps felt I had alluded to the fragility of his rule. I had the sense of sitting in an Islamic court before a grand vizier: loose words I uttered could be misinterpreted, as if we spoke in poems. The aide-de-camp became emotional beside the general's huddled form. He moaned and stammered, "What will happen to the people of the *grand boubou*?"

I did not understand the term *grand boubou*. He touched his *kaftan*. "Now is the time," the general said, speaking at last, "to reconcile Christians and Muslims and build a government of unity."

Having gained power through violence, the general, like many leaders who ruled unjustly, now invoked peace. Peace was the government's way of justifying more violence. Peace represented its victory, and would confirm the rebels' defeat. Peace allowed the government to hold on to power. And peace could be sold to the world, persuading it to send soldiers and foreign aid to maintain the current order. But such an imposed peace had to be continually enforced through aggression. Such peace endured only so long as power was monopolized.

General Kalil ordered his aide-de-camp to fetch a wedding photo album. He flipped through its giant pages, showing me pictures of him handing out "National Reconciliation Prizes" to schoolchildren. One picture showed him sweeping a yard. "I'm building the country," he said. "How many soldiers do you know who give up their guns to use a broom?" I was quiet; and he perhaps felt I did not absorb his meaning. "I worry that all of this"—he gestured at the land around him—"is going to burn."

I left the general's villa. In his driveway his chauffeur slept at the wheel of a black Mercedes. I assumed General Kalil had plundered this car, the villa, and the state's money when his forces seized power. The suddenness of his coming into wealth and power perhaps also gave him a sense of his position's instability: all this could be taken away just as easily.

I had intuited the general's fear of a hollow victory.

That night, at the church, a fever grew inside me. My body responded to suppressed fear. It didn't surprise me. I had routinely fallen sick as a boy before exams; and as a journalist, while waiting in a Congolese town for an attack; and in Rwanda when I learned a government spy tailed me. Now I shivered, sweated. My joints hurt against the thin mattress. I didn't know if I could leave in the morning. My mind ran amok. I worried I had displeased General Kalil, drawn him into his anxiety, made a powerful man expose his weakness. Out in the countryside, we would be at the mercy of soldiers.

My church room had two beds, one on either side, for traveling missionary companions. The shower was curtained off. I sat under the open tap, over the drain, water flowing down my head. And I tasted the streams of sweat flowing off my sticky hair.

Dripping over the floor, I rummaged in my knapsack, then emptied it. I had packed meticulously in Canada, but forgotten to put in, of all things, a towel. I used the spare bed's sheets to wipe myself down. I left the soaked sheets on the floor in a lump.

We convened in the parking lot at 4:00 a.m. for our last checks. "*L'essence?* Petrol?" "Yes, our barrel is full!" "Our gear?" "One, two . . . six bags!" "Did someone check the road is still open?" Bangui was closed off from 10:00 p.m. to 5:00 a.m., for security. "It's about to open!" Suleiman turned his key; the engine settled into a growl. He cruised up to National Highway 1 and Bangui's edge. Then he blasted us out of the capital, into the night.

We left behind Bangui's comforting isolation, its ignorance, elegant hotels, and tranquil neighborhoods. We could still, from here, retreat into the capital. This thought consoled me. I watched the land rush by.

We passed statues of women braiding their hair. I noticed them flash past, in a field.

"Women's rights?" I said to Thierry.

"*Reconciliation nationale,*" he replied. For the conflicts between people of the savannah and the river, and of the north and the south. The Republic had suffered five coups d'état and various foul play since its independence from France in 1960. Barthélemy Boganda, the country's independence hero, had died in a mysterious plane crash, some say planned by the French. His successor, David Dacko, was ousted in 1965. His successor, Jean-Bédel Bokassa, was ousted in 1979 by the French, who flew Dacko back to Bangui and reinstalled him as president. Dacko was ousted a second time by General André Kolingba, who organized elections in which Ange-Félix Patassé was elected, only to be himself ousted in 2003 by the former army chief of staff François Bozizé, who was then overthrown by the Seleka rebellion in 2013. For decades, the country had been in a state of perpetual rebellion.

"Women are the peacemakers?" I asked.

"It's more abstract," Thierry said. "Each tress represents a different identity." The sculpture was profound. Women embraced strands of identity as the necessary elements to create a peaceful union.

"Something's wrong," Suleiman said.

All of us noticed, at once, that people had disappeared from the highway. The emptiness was a sign of danger. But we didn't know why, and there was no one to ask. We were now already far from Bangui. Suleiman sped up in case road bandits planned an ambush.

Thierry held his voice recorder in his lap, expecting at any moment to come upon news.

"Rebels," Suleiman said.

"So close to Bangui?" I asked.

"They're violent."

I said, "But the government burns the villages."

"No, it's the dry season. Thatch roofs catch fire spontaneously." Suleiman's voice quivered.

Lewis glanced at me from the front seat.

So we had discovered that our driver was a government supporter. I quickly pacified Suleiman, saying, "The government is doing a difficult job."

A roadblock appeared and soldiers waved us to a stop. They demanded our *ordre de mission*: a one-page relic of the colonial French bureaucracy that listed our names, our purpose for traveling, and our vehicle's license plate number, all stamped and signed by the country's police chief. Lewis had arranged it for us in Bangui. Human Rights Watch's heft, and its ties to the U.S. government, had helped us obtain this permission to travel through the war.

Roadblocks, one by one, registered our passage toward Gaga. We collected a pink receipt for each payment.

"What's happening at Gaga?" Lewis asked the soldier collecting our money.

"Where's that?" he said.

"Never heard of it," said the soldier at our next checkpoint.

I reached behind my head, in the boot, and grabbed a

box of LU *Petit Écolier* milk chocolate cookies, which we'd bought at the supermarket in Bangui. I passed it around. We bit into the stacks of four cookies, consumed the box, and then another. I piled up the empty boxes, playing solemn despite being high, again, on the sugar.

We passed a torture center named Guantanamo, after the U.S. military prison in Cuba. Thierry said it was notorious, and Lewis described it as a hell where prisoners were held in deep pits that contained scorpion nests. From the highway we saw its cement buildings surrounded by palm trees.

Suleiman stopped at a restaurant to ask if it was safe. The diners, over plates of *meshwi*—grilled meat seasoned with chili powder—told us soldiers had passed here a week before. So we drove on, and asked again at the next town. We divined the war and gauged our distance from it.

Now we approached Yaloke, the city that served as the gateway to Gaga. The highway continued ahead, disappearing up over a hill. In my mind, I described to Nat the trees, earth, sky, the road moving swiftly beneath, and the bush, *la brousse*, speeding by. We couldn't see past where the road hit the horizon.

Gaga lay a short distance north. And the town of Yaloke was lit yellow. Oil lamps hung from shop awnings on its main drag. Pickup trucks transporting soldiers threw up a dusty haze. Soldiers ambled around in open-toe leather sandals. Shops blared heavy electronic music from loudspeakers. At one shop I bought myself a towel, and a local checkered scarf, of the kind soldiers wrapped around their faces.

I saw only men. A hotel receptionist told me that the soldiers kept the women indoors, for their pleasure. His hotel, like the others, was fully booked. A soldier guarding the staircase, chewing some stimulant, smiled at me as if I'd been let in on their secret.

Thierry knew of a school on Yaloke's outskirts, the Lycée Évangelique des Frères de Yaloke. Suleiman got directions, and drove us to its gates. Inside, children yelled and played basketball on a cement court. They were brazen, oblivious to the war. This school was a sanctuary, a paradise that almost seemed unjust, unsavory, and immune to the violence.

The school's principal showed us around his premises. The war had not touched the school, he said, though it had ravaged his entire province. We walked through this island of juvenile joy. The principal had negotiated with soldiers and extracted a promise that the children would not be touched. Soldiers still arrived at the school; each time the principal stepped out, unarmed, to negotiate with them.

A schoolteacher allowed us to sleep in his house. We rolled out the mattresses we had bought in PK5, Bangui's open-air-market neighborhood, and hung our mosquito nets from windows' metal frames. I showered. My brand-new towel hardly dried me off. The principal, like everyone so far, refused to comment on Gaga. But he showed Suleiman the way.

That night, I called Nat on the satellite phone.

"How are things at home?"

"Raphaëlle has the colic," she said. "I hardly sleep."

"She must've inherited it from me," I said. "I'll ask my mother to send you a British remedy, a syrup called Doctor something . . ."

"Where are you?"

"Almost at Gaga." I told her Thierry had received a report of a massacre, and how no one spoke to us about this place.

She said, "Call me when you get to it."

I then called my mother, asking her to check on Raphaëlle, and in the morning we left Yaloke, heading north, into the jungle. Trees crowded our vehicle and thudded against our roof and windows, the branches bending and swinging into us. The tiring percussion lasted about half an hour. Suddenly the foliage opened up and we emerged out on a hilltop. This was Gaga. We had reached the front line.

Smoke rose from the jungle in columns. Mortar bombs made resonant explosions. Suleiman parked at a white-washed building, the government base. A rumble startled us: three soldiers drove motorcycles down the hill. A soldier pointed us to a giant mango tree. The base's commander gave his name as Yusuf and ordered his men to draw us chairs.

I declined the seat, and asked Yusuf's permission to follow the soldiers on motorcycles down the hill.

Lewis wanted to interview Yusuf about the battle. So I would have to go alone. Yusuf seemed not to care; he took off his camouflage cap, rubbed his forehead, and waved me down.

Lewis asked when I'd return.

I collected my notebook and cash from our vehicle. "It's safer here, with the government," Suleiman said. But I felt we would learn little under Yusuf's protection. Suleiman took up position at the truck, in case we needed to leave in a hurry. Thierry told me not to walk too far away. He showed me how to orient myself by the hills, so I knew my way back. He showed me this consideration, and said he would have joined me but needed to assist Lewis. Our cell phones did not catch the network here, so Lewis declared the parking lot as our rendezvous point. He pointed at his feet and looked up at me: "You hear me? Come back to this place."

Cracks ran across the yellow hill. I followed the valleys made by rainwater flowing down, hopping from little ridge to ridge until I got over to its other side. I reached Gaga's outskirts, and circled past its houses. A pit was filled with white fluid and reeked of chemical. I peered inside it. This was how health authorities disinfected mass graves.

From behind a house I heard a noise, which I followed, through an alley, to find myself in a procession of people.

They fled Gaga through an opening in the jungle wall, into its darkness. Gunfire sounded in bursts. These people walked straight into the conflict. I asked a man in the procession why. He said Gaga's residents expected another massacre. They fled before it started, escaping Yusuf, the government commander on the hilltop.

Parents gently nudged children ahead, their babies tied tight to their backs, the babies' cheeks pressed flat against the spines. They had taken apart their homes; on their heads, they carried cooking pots and rolled-up tin roofs.

A cobbler squatted on our path, and people gathered around him holding broken slippers. The jungle terrain was harsh, but safer than the roads. The cobbler sewed frantically, working thick cord and rubber—he was this battle's hero. People urged him to hurry up so they could flee.

I reached the jungle's edge; I turned toward the hilltop, where Lewis, Thierry, and Suleiman waited, then I joined in the procession. A tall man beside me stumbled. I grabbed his casserole but he refused my help.

"The anti-balaka"—the rebels—I said, guessing at where the people were headed.

He pointed ahead.

I had left my home, then Bangui, and now my team. At each stage I had not been prevented from venturing farther. Most important, Nat had not stopped me; she had instead encouraged me. Home was a haven, a retreat, and a place I could leave. I needed home, and also needed, almost constantly, to leave it, and her.

Nat and I had walked together to an unlit part of Congo's border with Rwanda—through a dark like in this place. We had come upon a soldier in a hammock, a burning cigarette butt in his mouth and a rifle in his lap. The soldier had not answered our questions; in silence Nat and I had stared at a volcano's red glow, and at the yellow lights of the houses across the border.

I smelled the smoke. The bombs resonated like thunder. The noise made me instinctively look up to see the sun hanging in the blue sky, like a jewel.

Our procession reached a stream.

A teenager up to his ankles in the water stopped me. "I saw you in Gaga," he said. "Talking to people."

"I'm reporting on the massacre," I said.

"My name is Moussumba, Jean Noël." He said the name solemnly, formally. "I'll take you inside where we can talk about it."

I tried hopping over the pebbles in the stream. "No shoes," Jean Noël said. "Come barefoot."

So I tied together my sneakers' laces and hung them over my shoulder. I stuffed my socks into my pockets. Jean Noël moved fast. The stones and broken twigs pressed painfully into my feet.

Only a few steps inside with him, and I was lost. Light filtered in through the jungle canopy, casting a pattern of shadows over our bodies. The bombs sounded more terrifying; the gunfire came as a succession of hisses, a rattle moving to and fro across our range of hearing.

I heard voices from within the trees—when I tried to peer inside, people yelled at me. "Don't look!" Jean Noël shouted. "Don't look at where the people are hiding!" We ran through alleyways hacked out through the jungle. Gaga's residents had built a new, hidden city here. It had no signposts. The paths did not bear names. This city's addresses were secret. The people of Gaga no longer found security in openness, or in community. So Gaga had been turned inside out, and families now sought isolation, the refuge of anonymity. No wonder this massacre had been so hard to track down. Its survivors had retreated within.

I was suddenly forced off my path and into the trees by a woman holding a bed frame over her head.

"Maman," I said.

She said, "Help us, son."

Two kilometers farther inside, the blasts rang in my ears, and we passed men carrying guns sitting on the forest floor and tying bandages over fresh wounds. Their white gauze was covered in dust and dried blood. They were rebel fighters, the secretive anti-balaka.

We approached the fighting.

Dirt stuck to my face and lodged in my tear glands. I stung my eyes with my soiled hands.

Suddenly, Jean Noël's family emerged in a clearing. His father insisted on serving me tea, that I should stay awhile. With the shooting as our backdrop, he poured tea out of a thermos into a cup, and showed me his half-built home, a dome-shaped structure made of branches and large leaves.

"What kind of leaves?"

"*Bakwa*," he said, "from a flowering tree."

Inside his home, the gunshots sounded muffled. I crawled over his bed of leaves, beneath his possessions hidden among the branches: a toothbrush, a Bible, and three batteries bound by a rubber band and connected to a naked bulb.

Jean Noël's father and brother told me, as we sipped from melamine cups, that the massacre had made Gaga "*sinistré*"—a disaster zone. Soldiers had killed a hundred young men to warn the rebels not to resist. They had gone house to house, and shot those who had fled. "They left our streets littered with cadavers."

"They slit our throats like animals."

The father said he had hidden his motorcycle and guns behind these trees. He prepared a counterattack. He swore they would take back Gaga, that the rebels would win.

He named each person in the clearing for my benefit, touching them one by one: Moussumba Abdias . . . Moussumba Roustam . . . Moussumba Jean Noël. He made sure I spelled their names right, as though afraid that in hiding their names had lost meaning and risked being forgotten. I had finished my tea.

Again I fell behind Jean Noël—he moved faster on our return. I tripped over the roots. The ground was covered in plastic: empty sachets of alcohol and "Tom Tom" toffee wrappers stamped into the dirt. People used alcohol and toffee to kill their hunger, so they didn't have to stop for food, and could cover longer distances.

At the stream where I had found Jean Noël, I sat on a boulder and put on my socks and shoes.

"Be careful with those men," he said.

I walked through Gaga, now a ghost town. The streets were deserted. Many houses were locked; their doors were painted bright yellow, blue, and red.

Occasionally I saw a man sit on his porch; only the Muslims had dared stay behind.

Rockets sounded behind me, one after the other, four in all. The smoke now rose from the forest closer to Gaga. The battle would soon reach us. I started to jog up.

But my path was blocked by pigs. They ambled in groups on the street. They looked up at me. I ducked inside a house, but they were in here. Pigs ate vegetables in the house's storeroom, lay on the bed and grunted, and made love on the kitchen floor. The pigs had replaced the people. I tried to circumvent them, but they blocked me. I gingerly nudged my way through their group. Yusuf's soldiers had seized all the goats and chickens from these houses, but being Muslims they had not touched the pigs. So the war had set the pigs free.

The hill glowed ochre. I ran up, like an animal exposed, suddenly feeling alone, relieved when I reached the government base and saw everyone still sitting there. I grabbed a white plastic chair and rested in the shade of the mango tree.

Yusuf was irritated. He interrogated a large man.

I nudged Lewis. "Who is that?"

"Gaga's prefect," he said. "Name is Simplice."

"And what's the problem?"

"Yusuf thinks Simplice knows where the rebels are hiding."

"You think we're safe here? I saw a mass grave down the hill, a pit filled with white disinfectant."

"Take out your notebook," Yusuf ordered Simplice.

He dictated: "I wish my citizens joy." And he watched Simplice write out the words. "Our soldiers are about to win this battle. Everyone should stay indoors until I order that they should leave. Anyone caught outside will be arrested as a rebel sympathizer . . ."

"But colonel," I said to Yusuf. "The people have already left Gaga. The city is empty."

"Where will they go?" he said, "Only the jungle, and they will return."

"The rebels are almost here."

"So let them come up here. If I have to shoot them myself, I'll do it!"

Yusuf had no plan, besides making a brave stand against the rebels. And sitting beside him, our team looked like his collaborators. But the smoke was still where it had been; it had not drawn closer.

A soldier pushed a ragged, unkempt man toward us and declared him a spy. The man's hands were bound behind his back. The prisoner pleaded that he knew no rebels. "You have the wrong man," he said. Yusuf dispatched him to a room in the government building, followed by a boy soldier holding a whip, whose long black rubber strips were intertwined with sharp metal wires.

The whip's cracks sounded from the room, and the man's screams, his begging. Yusuf laughed. "He will need antibiotics after this." But such specialized medication was hard to find in the war. Without them, wounds and lacerations could cost a man a limb.

The boy returned, strutting, and looking sideways, as if soliciting applause from Yusuf's men. Holding his whip in his left hand, he offered me a handshake. He said, "Tony Montana," in an affected Italian accent. Repulsed by all the screams, I nodded. But Tony frowned. "You don't know that movie?"

His voice had not cracked. He was maybe thirteen years old.

"I want to be *méchant*," he said. "Cruel, like Al Pacino in *Scarface*."

I worried I had annoyed him. But he pulled up a chair next to mine, and started to scroll on his smartphone. He showed me pictures of women, Hollywood celebrities in skimpy outfits for magazine photoshoots. "Look at how they dress," he said, "these whores, *les putes*."

"You've had this kind of woman?" And he smiled, showing me his perfect teeth.

"Here," Yusuf said, and he handed me his rifle. "Do you know how to use it?" I shook my head. He showed me how to disarm its safety, so the rifle was live. It was a FAMAS, the French army's standard-issue assault rifle.

"You want to shoot the prisoner?" he said.

I looked uneasy. He laughed.

I asked if he'd gotten the rifle in France.

The Seleka bought it, he said. "In Dubai, at the *souq*."

"I grew up in Dubai."

"Dubai," he said, making his eyes large. "The world's richest Muslim city, like Baghdad or Constantinople used to be."

The FAMAS in my lap, I relaxed. The sky was cloudless. The bombs had suddenly stopped. Yusuf and Tony looked bored. Simplice slouched in his chair, holding a sheaf: his manifesto for peace. Lewis wrote in his notebook. Thierry seized the lull for a nap, his head nodding against his shoulder.

We waited for the battle to restart, like the background music for a party. It seemed too hot to fight now—that was why they had stopped. I shared a cigarette with the soldier beside me, and learned that the scowling dark man hunched behind Yusuf was a Sudanese poacher. He oversaw a second set of massacres, which Lewis and I didn't investigate: of forest elephants. The country's southwest was one of these elephants' last refuges. But they were killed for ivory to exchange for guns. The soldier beside me said, "Can you bring me a digger from Dubai?" "A digger?" "An earth digger," he said, "to excavate this hill." "Why?" "Gold," he said, pointing at the eastern slope. "As payment, I'll give you all the gold on this side of this hill."

At that moment, a pickup truck burst over the hilltop and pierced the silence. Armed boys on its back wore necklaces of bullets and sunglasses. Their faces and arms were scarred. Government reinforcements had arrived. The boys jumped off the truck and huddled to protect the officer stepping out of its cab.

"General Hamad!" The soldiers all saluted a burly man wearing an olive green uniform and black leather sandals. But as soon as he stepped out he screamed at Yusuf, "Are you a soldier? How many men have you sent in?"

Yusuf, holding a salute, said, "Fifteen."

"Are you really a soldier?" he yelled, disdainfully. "You've sent fifteen men to their deaths."

I had been correct that the rebels were winning, that they were closing in on us, and that Yusuf had no sensible strategy.

The general set out to meet the rebels. He and Yusuf marched down the hill with their troops. I motioned to Lewis and Thierry that we should follow them.

A family then drove up the hill, past Yusuf and Hamad, on a motorcycle stacked high with casseroles. They pleaded with a soldier to pass. But the soldiers confiscated their motorcycle and told them to continue on foot. The family now stacked their casseroles on their heads.

I set off downhill. Behind me, Tony took over the base, ordering soldiers twice his age to rearrange the chairs and be still. "We need some quiet," Tony said. "Why are we talking so much?"

A soldier said, "Who is talking here?"

"Do you want a whipping?" said Tony. He sat in his chair and dismantled his AK-47 rifle, undoing its springs, irritated, trying to jam a bullet into a cartridge already full.

"I need to think how we will win," he said, "or by this night we will all be killed."

We crossed over the deep ridges of the ochre hill. Some people, mostly Muslim, gathered and followed us. The general stopped in Gaga's marketplace. He raised his arm, pointed at the sky, and shouted: "Is there any Islam here?"

He shouted again, "I will attack the anti-balaka."

The Muslims left and returned with yellow canisters and motorbikes. We witnessed a scene of military procurement in the war. Soldiers swirled around us, grabbing money and food. People formed a queue to solemnly pour petrol into the motorcycles' tanks. The market filled with fumes.

General Hamad climbed onto a motorcycle, crushing its suspension under his weight, and drove in a convoy into the hidden jungle city. Yusuf stayed behind to defend Gaga. I instinctively followed the general along the dirt path. But one of his soldiers stood guard, wearing camouflage pants and a dirty white singlet.

I said in French, "I'm with the general."

He shook his head because he didn't understand. "*Aarabiya?*"

"Sorry, no Arabic," I said. "No French?"

"Sorry, no French."

"Sango?" It was the official Central African language.

"No Sango."

He wasn't from here.

"English?" I offered as a last resort.

He slapped my back and said, "My friend. My name is Colonel Aktahir and I come from Sudan!" So we spoke in the language of the new colonizer, of the foreigners who occupied this land. General Hamad and the elephant poacher were both from Sudan.

"You can't go in," the soldier said. "Who will guarantee your safety?"

"I will write about how the general wins."

"No entry."

"The general doesn't want us to see?" I said.

I left, and after a few steps turned. Colonel Aktahir waited in the same place, watching me.

In Gaga, I ran into Jean Noël, who sat on the edge of a cemetery dug for some victims of the recent massacre. He spoke softly: "General Hamad is going to four towns. Dombourou, Carrefour, Zoé, and Camp Bangui." The last town was named after the capital, itself named after the Ubangi River.

The people in those towns secretly helped the rebels, and the general had found them out. Still, the general was outnumbered with thirty-five men against perhaps three hundred. And so, as it had been since the war's beginning, to capture and hold on to power, the government would have to be brutal in order to win. Gaga had already dispatched messengers to warn them of the impending assault.

I told Jean Noël that Colonel Aktahir, one of General Hamad's men, had blocked my passage. Jean Noël said I could try a different route, that there was a road to Gaga's west, which the soldiers did not use, and might not even know of, many of them being foreigners. Even Yusuf was from the country's south.

"You can only walk on this road," Jean Noël said, "or maybe go by motorbike."

"How long is the journey?"

Jean Noël said he didn't know, maybe a few hours. But Jean Noël's friend, sitting beside him, said it would take a day. Another villager said that it would take fifty hours. Jean Noël got up to return to his father, in the jungle.

Lewis had meanwhile gathered evidence of Gaga's massacre from Simplice and others—to a degree that it could be presented in a court.

We got into our pickup.

Simplice called out to me, ran up to our truck, and, breathless, said he would transmit to us news about the general's killings. That night, he would walk up a hillock just outside Gaga to catch the cell phone network.

Suleiman drove us out.

Back at the school, Lewis turned on his satellite phone, but as soon as he connected to the Internet, several large files started to download and jam our line. We wondered if Human Rights Watch had sent us satellite images of attacks.

We opened the first photograph. It was an extremely high-resolution baby picture that had consumed our bandwidth. Lewis called home to tell Niccola, his wife, that our Internet connection was too slow to send baby pictures. "I know, I miss you too," he said. And he showed us those photos. "Look at my boy. And that's my beautiful wife." He spoke like a man for whom what was supposed to happen had finally happened. A family—something he'd waited for. He spoke as if he had finally done right.

"I'm a lucky man."

And we all agreed.

Lewis wrote up a brief about the massacre, mentioning the mass grave with disinfectant that I had found, and sent it to his office in New York. Human Rights Watch would relay his information, in an official complaint, to the Central African government and, in a separate report, to the governments of the United States and France—which, as the former colonial power was still seen as "responsible" for the chaos here—and the Secretary General of the United Nations. Together the world would threaten to withdraw financial aid and international peacekeepers from the Central African Republic if such massacres did not stop.

That was our journey's first success. We had documented Gaga's massacre and informed authorities in Bangui and abroad, thus making it part of the official international record of this war. I began my magazine piece with the scene of people fleeing Gaga for their secret jungle city.

We had absorbed, in a single day, a massacre, the battle, and the general's counterattack. After Lewis filed his report, Thierry shared pictures of his fiancée. He was saving up to pay his wedding. His salary from our journey would help. I pulled out a photograph of Raphaëlle that Nat had stuffed into my wallet before I had left. My daughter wore a woolen hat on her way home from hospital, right after her birth.

Was it the fear and risk of that day which made me, again, seek out the comfort of my home? I rushed to call Nat and tell her all that had happened. From my arriving at the front line to the walk with Jean Noël. How General Hamad left Gaga to assault four towns with only thirty-five men. The Sudanese mercenary who'd prevented me from pursuing him. That we now tried to follow the general along a separate route. "Hello?" I said. The line was silent; I thought I had lost her. Then I heard Raphaëlle cry. "I have to go," Nat said, and she hung up. Her landline, disconnected in Shippagan, buzzed my ear.

On returning to our room, I realized we had developed a new bond, as a team. We could have panicked in Gaga. An ease had developed among us, putting the disquiet from home out of my mind.

That night, Lewis approached me as we brushed our teeth on the Yaloke school's football field.

He said, "I'm worried."

Pulling my brush out of my foaming mouth, I asked about what.

"Hamad."

His teeth shone, reflecting the stray light. We rinsed our

mouths with water from large red mugs that a teacher had given us, and spat out the foam so it glowed on the grass.

"Hamad's men might have tracked us here from Gaga," Lewis said.

We walked back inside and each lay on a slim mattress under a mosquito net set up like a tent. Mosquitoes managed to prick me through my net. Lewis asked about Raphaëlle; he said Niccola wanted another child, and his mother more grandchildren. "It isn't so easy traveling once you have kids."

"We have work tomorrow," I said.

I was woken by footsteps at first light. Students giggled outside my window. The team was up. We rolled up our mattresses and nets and stowed them in the pickup's back. We discussed our route, to pursue Hamad. Gaga remained our best option.

The base was silent now. Morose soldiers sat under the mango tree. Simplice looked worried, and stole a glance at us. He had never called me with his report, as he had promised. But we couldn't converse.

"I don't know if Simplice is loyal to me," Yusuf said.

It was a threat.

"Tell me," Yusuf cajoled him.

He was forcing Simplice to betray the rebels' locations. Tony Montana sat hunched over his legs, his metal wire whip hanging off a tree.

"My best fighter," Yusuf said, gesturing at Tony.

"But he's just a boy," I said.

"He's fearless. The men, I have to feed them drugs. Tony fights without drugs."

Tony smiled.

As if emboldened, and asking something he'd held back, he said to me, "Can you find me a woman? A white, *une blanche?*"

"Can we go down?" I asked Yusuf.

He said all of Gaga was off-limits, and we should leave.

Another place in the country had closed up to outside observers; and another road on the country's map could not be traveled. Yusuf said we could call him for the general's official communiqué. The view, on that day, was picturesque, and peaceful. The forest canopy stretched to the horizon; birds flew overhead. I heard pigs grunt.

I wrote in my notebook in a scrawl, my hand flying over the page, thrown by the bumps on Gaga's red laterite road. We hit the highway, and sped ahead smoothly over the asphalt.

From time to time we stopped to interview people walking or eating at a restaurant, but they did not want to speak about General Hamad's killings.

"He launched his attack from Gaga," I said to one man.

I spotted no reaction in his eyes. "Another attack," he said, and shrugged.

It took us until the fourth town that we passed on the highway to find someone who would speak of the attack.

Bekadili's prefect was a slender man. He wore a frayed black suit jacket on which he had pinned a brooch of the country's multicolored flag: blue, white, green, yellow, and red. Blue represented the sky, white peace, green hope, yellow tolerance, and the red stripe running across the other colors: the blood of the independence martyrs. The prefect's spectacles were held together by white tape. He blinked at us through his thick lenses.

"Wait three days," he said, "until the soldiers leave."

He would not utter the general's name.

"But the attack is happening now," I said.

"That's the problem."

A government convoy then arrived at Bekadili, and a general—from the stars on his lapels—stepped out of a truck.

Lewis muttered, "I told you they were tracking us."

The general introduced himself as Ali, and stepped into Bekadili's communal thatch hut—its *majlis*—where he inspected our *ordre de mission*.

"Is that your vehicle?" he said, pointing at Suleiman's pickup parked on the roadside. He checked its plate number. After a while he said that our papers were in order.

We waited for his convoy to drive away. Was it luck? It seemed unbelievable. I thought it strange that a general, and not a lower-ranked officer, had taken the time to personally verify our papers. It hadn't happened at any of the roadblocks or anywhere else.

"If we get shot," Lewis said, "they'll just say it was an

accident on the front line." He was right that such a claim would be difficult for investigators to disprove.

The prefect was spooked.

"What do we do from here?" I said. "Turn back? Go forward?"

The prefect brought out some Castel beer, and a Coca-Cola for Suleiman. "Sorry," the prefect said, "I have no ice to offer." The five of us leaned back on the *majlis*'s parapet walls, resting in its shade and sipping warm drinks.

REBELLION

Blocked from investigating Hamad's attack, we looked further west, to a relatively remote part of the country. There had been a spate of killings in that area.

And in coming to Bekadili we had already traveled halfway to the alleged locations of those killings in the Yadé massif, a granite highland about three hundred meters above Bekadili, studded with granite peaks called *kaga*.

The capital of the *préfecture*—an administrative region similar to a province or state, where these new killings were reported—was called Bouar. The French had made this city a military garrison in 1907, though it had been, for about five years around World War I, occupied by Germans. The French finally abandoned this strategic site in 1978, nearly two decades after their colonial rule ended.

This préfecture, called Nana-Mambéré, had a long history of rebellion against tyranny. It had been the site of the infamous "War of the Hoe Handle" (or the Kongo-Wara revolt) in 1928, when fifty thousand Central Africans, armed with their hoes and farm tools, fought a thousand

French soldiers and resisted for two years by retreating to the plateau's caves, until their rebellion was brutally put down. These caves were now used by the anti-balaka rebels, who thus continued their intermittent habitation from three thousand years before. A Stone Age civilization had placed giant rocks across the highland, many five meters high, like those at Stonehenge, likely to record their astronomical calculations. The government killings we investigated had forced the anti-balaka rebels into hiding.

I sent Nat an SMS: "Change in plans. We're heading to Bouar, *nous allons a Bouar.*"

I wondered if she would look up the city or its location. With Raphaëlle's colic flaring up, Nat hardly slept.

In any case, she didn't reply.

I felt it was unnecessary to tell her about the new reports of killings in the west, or that our team traveled across the country to investigate them. She now cared for Raphaëlle on behalf of us both, taking complete responsibility for our child's life, anticipating her every urgent and vital need, divining why she was crying. A child induced so much anxiety.

I waited, sent another SMS: *je t'aime.* I called, but she didn't pick up after three rings and so I hung up flustered and focused on the road ahead.

The reports of killings now drew us northwest from Bekadili, over a no-man's-land, to Bossemptele, a major crossroads, where we switched from National Highway 1 to National Highway 3. "The shootouts have started inside Bouar," Thierry said, relaying messages from his local colleagues. The news bulletins had so far not reported on the violence in Bouar. News passed by word of mouth, among friends.

At each town Suleiman stopped and asked passersby, "Is the route ahead safe?" Through the empty areas he drove hard. Our petrol sloshed around in the barrel behind us.

The blue sky met our road's infinite asphalt line on the horizon. Low shrubs spread out on both sides as we climbed into the Yadé massif. My eyes became strained from staring at the flatlands: we searched for signs of the *zaraguinas*, otherwise known as the *"coupeurs de route,"* or "road cutters." These freelance armed bandits mounted highway ambushes and were particularly dangerous at this moment, near the end of the rainy season, when the roads opened up.

The anti-balaka rebellion traced its origins to people's militias, armed with homemade weapons, which villages and towns had created to protect themselves from the *zaraguinas*. Such militias had been essential in the absence of state protection, and became even more vital now that the state turned on its people.

We overtook a bush lorry, a mode of public transport on these highways. An old Berliet lorry lurched from side to side, not allowing Suleiman to overtake. Passengers sat high atop its cargo. And the lorry was covered in bicycles, reed baskets, and yellow *bidons*: canisters of petrol hanging from hooks on the lorry's body. It was a risky journey, in the war. But people still needed to trade goods and earn their living, or bring help to their families, or flee the violence. Suleiman finally found a gap to overtake, and as we made our pass I flashed a thumbs-up at the driver, who nodded as he wrestled with his steering wheel to hold the rocking lorry steady.

A lone figure, a silhouette, appeared ahead. Suleiman's hands hesitated, and he began to tap on the brake pedal so we accelerated and slowed. I clutched at my armrests. It could be a trap, to make us slow down: a *zaraguina* setup to ambush us. The figure now crossed the road. We got near it, and Suleiman rashly accelerated. But it was only a boy. He played on the road, whipping a bicycle wheel rim with a branch to drive it forward and keep it balanced. A second lonely figure appeared on the horizon.

This turned out to be an old man on a bicycle.

"In this heat," I murmured.

The man pedaled slowly, his weight shifting to a side, then the other, as each leg came down.

We trained our eyes on the road, a hot current rising over it in waves and distorting our vision. We became silent from the stress, and when it was unbearable, Suleiman reached forward. He flipped a dial and turned on some music, enveloping us in a man's melodic wails.

He played his music off a flash drive. The relaxation felt false, a result of cutting us off from the surrounding danger.

I said, "Shouldn't we listen to the news?"

But Suleiman was silent.

I repeated: "Can we get some news?"

"You won't find any here," he said, after a pause.

The government had destroyed most radio station antennae, especially in the areas they had attacked, to isolate people.

I turned the dial and filled our cab with loud static. Suleiman glanced over and smacked his lips, irritated. And the sound jarred. But eventually, I tuned in to the voice of a newsreader. Then immediately we lost the signal, and found ourselves again immersed in the grating static.

Suleiman reached over to the radio.

"Where from?" I said, of the man wailing again.

"Old folk songs."

"Central African?"

"From Chad."

"It's like the music from Dubai," I said, "where I grew up."

"I am from Chad," he said. "My parents still live there."

The road was empty again. I looked out at the passing shrubland. We drove through this countryside as four blind men, ignorant of what happened even a few meters off our road. It was too dangerous to make detours for tourism.

"Idriss Déby has sent soldiers to fight for the government," I said, referring to the Chadian president, a kingmaker throughout Central Africa, including this country.

"This whole country was once Muslim," Suleiman said.

The music turned pleasant, the wails giving to a romantic ballad.

We passed manioc fields, signs of a village nearby. A

hardy crop from Brazil, introduced to this country by the French, it could survive without upkeep for months. A century before, it was an ideal crop for Central African men forced to leave home for long periods, to work as porters and slaves for colonial French companies. And it remained useful for people on the move, who now fled the war. Rich in sugar but lacking other nutrients, manioc was served fried, boiled, fermented as a heavy cake called *chikwang*, or as a powder kneaded into dough called *gozo*, eaten with the fingers in bite-sized balls. In these forms, manioc constituted nearly 90 percent of the local diet.

We stopped on the roadside for a bathroom break, and when Lewis and I had walked behind a tree, against the sound of our urine slapping into the mud, I said to him, "Maybe, while Suleiman is around us, we should speak in code?"

"He knows we're investigating the government's killings." Lewis seemed testy. He had noticed, I thought.

"It's of course more dangerous if Suleiman can understand everything we say."

"Nothing we're doing is illegal," Lewis said uncertainly. "We have government permission."

"And if we cross a line, to somewhere the government wouldn't want us to be?"

"How about the Seattle Mariners," he suggested, "for the Seleka, the government."

"He'll wise up if we talk too much about baseball."

"The anti-balaka," he went on, "can be the Boston Red Sox."

We zipped ourselves up and returned to our truck.

"The Red Sox are in position to attack," Lewis said, now sounding a little giddy. "But the Seattle Mariners are still in control of this inning."

At least we laughed.

Child soldiers rapped on our windows at these remote roadblocks. We handed them our *ordre de mission* and the toll fee. The soldiers here were also more ragged. The thatch on their huts drooped almost to the ground, so as to block the sun until it set over the Yadé massif. The child soldiers did not provide us pink receipts. And their manioc, spread out over the ground to dry, gave off a bitter smell. The roadblocks, one after the other, caused a traffic jam here in this empty zone, like it was rush hour.

Passengers climbed off a bush lorry parked diagonally at a roadblock, and the descending passengers then stripped at gunpoint. Over a mat before them lay money, jewelry, and medicines; and beside it, a pile of their clothes and underclothes. Soldiers gripped oranges between their teeth and made sucking noises at the women. The naked men waited to one side.

A few child soldiers loitered beside us, awaiting instructions from their commander. I offered them cigarettes. They shook their bodies to Suleiman's music, smiling and holding their cigarette butts between their lips. Suleiman shook in his seat with them. I, too, made a little dance.

We passed a petrol station burnt right up to its skeletal

frame. The scorched metal, now thin like paper, slowly blew off in the wind. The government had also burned petrol stations on their march to capture Bangui, so their enemies were stranded behind them. The countryside was starved of fuel. Escape became expensive. Journeys were riskier.

A man sat in this petrol station's shade, selling tubers.

"*Kalongo*," he said, offering me a bag.

I asked what it was.

"An aphrodisiac," Thierry said.

I bought some of the carrot-like yellow root.

The arousal it produced, a tingling sensation, was stimulating, profound. The root invaded my thoughts with eroticism. And I desired an embrace, a physical solace, as I can suddenly require after a period of fear, and when I am far from home.

In Bouar, the former French military garrison, we asked about the rebels.

"Look west," people said.

A woman pointed. "They're waiting inside the caves."

But the plateau's boulders and shadows confused my eye. The rebels benefited from this natural camouflage.

We drove past the source of the Lobaye River, which flowed east from a neighborhood in Bouar and then south into the Ubangi River. To Bouar's west were the Nana and Mambéré rivers, which gave their names to this préfecture, Nana-Mambéré. And to the north flowed a fourth river, called the Ouham. It was nearing the end of the rainy season, and the dry Harmattan winds had started to blow from the deserts toward Africa's western coast. The Harmattan was here believed to be a magical *fetish* wind that aided warriors. Central Africans in these parts called the wind the *Maigoro.*

Bouar, during colonial times, had been known as one of Central Africa's most desirable cities, offering French families direct flights to Paris, a cool high-altitude climate, and for the children, a prestigious *lycée*, a French public school.

We stayed at Bouar's imposing Cathédrale Saint-Joseph. A tank protected the cathedral's gates, where a plaque declared that this giant, octagonal structure, with its copper-laminate roof, shining above the city, had been built by Italian industrialists for their dead child. African soldiers milled about, outside the cathedral's gates, deployed here from Congo and Gabon for the African Union peacekeeping mission. Inside the cathedral, tall stained-glass windows made with Bohemia crystal—a plumb oxide granting them exceptional clarity—filtered in tinted colored light.

The abbot, "*le père blanc*" (or the white father), was a Polish Catholic priest named Mirek. We needed his advice, because anywhere north of the line drawn from Bouar and heading about thirty degrees north, all the way to the northeastern border with Sudan, was considered dangerous due to the *zaraguinas*, who operated in this zone with great impunity.

We lunched with Mirek in the cathedral's high-ceilinged

dining room. The abbot was bald and spoke almost in a whisper.

"In the morning I'll drive through the anti-balaka territory," he said.

This was north of Bouar, in an arid and rocky area that the rebels had occupied. Mirek's gold-rimmed glasses glinted against his pale, hairless face. And his starched, cream-colored shirt had been firmly ironed with creases along his sleeves.

"The rebels are Christian," he said. "So I don't think they will attack me."

He brought help to another priest, whose town, Bohong, had been sacked by soldiers. This was one of the killings Lewis had wanted to investigate. Soldiers there had killed dozens of people, at the very least, Mirek said, and they had shot at the church building. They had also stolen the church door. The altar now had no protection, nor the priest, and were exposed during all hours of the day and night.

"We don't accept that," Mirek said.

"Even in a town so remote," I said.

"I have to show the soldiers that our priest there, Michel," he said, sipping tea, "is not abandoned."

"Attacking a place of worship is illegal," Lewis said. "The soldiers violated the laws of war."

Mirek said, "I'll need to fix up a new door."

I asked if we could join the abbot's expedition. It would take us to another killing site, and through newly conquered rebel territory.

Mirek shrugged. "We meet at the front gate," he said, "at 5:00 a.m."

So our team now needed to rest.

I spent the evening in my bed, beneath a dim bulb. Mirek had installed solar panels; Bouar was not electrified. I washed my face in my room's sink; it was our first lodging since Bangui with running water—and here, brought right into the privacy of our rooms.

After dinner, our team drove out of the cathedral, through Bouar, to investigate the recent shootouts. We reached a neighborhood on the city's periphery. In the dark, it was difficult to find the house we sought.

In its courtyard, Lewis interviewed one of the only survivors of a shootout: a young woman wearing a sleeveless green shirt. Lewis cleared his throat. "My name is Lewis," he said.

"Ey." She looked at her feet.

"I will ask you some questions about what happened at the shootout." She nodded. "I won't use your name."

"Ey."

"Are you willing to speak to me?"

"Ey."

Lewis sat up. "*On est là.*"—We are ready. Lewis began each interview with this legally required preamble.

The government had killed a dozen people in that shootout, she said. Men, women, and children. The woman said that her friends, "Christian people," had hidden in a hut on a secluded farm. But a boy had escaped the hut and panicked. He spontaneously, and independently, confessed to the Muslim authorities that his family had helped the rebels. He then tried to save himself by betraying the others' location.

A hen jumped into the house and used its talon to scratch the floor.

Lewis said, seeming to think aloud, "Will you be safe?" We had found her by asking around in her neighborhood—too easily. She risked a reprisal as a shootout survivor.

She said, "Where will I go?"

"The cathedral," Lewis said.

The woman's courage, in speaking, had allowed us to document that shootout. Lewis had recorded her testimony for the international courts, and I for my magazine piece. The hen now pecked at the insects she had exposed in the mud.

Thierry helped us locate a man who had survived that same shootout. We phoned him. He asked us to come to a street in the city's center. There, illuminated by our pickup's headlights, the engine running, Lewis painstakingly corroborated the testimony of the woman we had just met: how many people had been in the hut and the time of day when the soldiers had shot at them. We ended up working late though we had wanted rest.

I woke up tired for our drive to the northern killing site, Bohong.

We traversed a rocky moonscape. Cell phone networks

didn't reach this place. And Suleiman, Lewis, and Thierry, in their vehicle, fell behind Mirek and me, in the abbot's white pickup. Lewis stopped to interview people about the shootout and other killings. Mirek was in a hurry.

Our doors rattled. My seat missed its cover, so I sat directly on the yellow, cratered foam. Mirek was missing his rearview and side mirrors. "*Tu vois bien*"—you see well— the abbot said, making a pun. In the pickup's back, Firmin, the church carpenter, sat atop a new door.

Our pickup suddenly started to squeak, alarming us. Mirek stopped and crawled to inspect the truck's undercarriage.

"Nothing looks broken," he said.

We drove on, the squeaking louder.

We crossed over a stone bridge, like one might find in old Europe, over the Ouham River, passing into the Ouham-Pendé préfecture. A sign said that Italian prisoners of war, captured during World War II, had built the bridge.

Mirek suddenly turned into a village and parked.

"They did not see me," he said. He honked.

The village was silent. Mirek pressed his palm on the steering wheel, sounding an extended honk. I saw a movement at the edge of my vision: a man ran at us. "Roll down your window!" Mirek shouted. The man knocked on my door. "Your window!" Mirek said. I rolled it down and the man thrust a sheet of paper at my face. He stuck his head inside our cab, and I felt his breaths over the hairs of my arm.

"*Merci, abbé.*"—Thank you, abbot, he said.

Mirek and he spoke in rapid-fire Sango. The villager shook his head. He gave Mirek a weary smile, and ran off through the huts.

We were alone.

I said, "A rebel?"

Mirek nodded. "Probably, by now," he said. "All the villagers are joining the rebels to fight against the government."

I turned toward Firmin, behind us.

"How long will your new door last against the soldiers?"

"I had this new one made with rosewood," Mirek said. It was an expensive wood. "If they take this, I'll come back with another one."

The rebel's sheet lay in my lap. On it, in neat handwriting with a ballpoint pen, columns had been drawn using a straightedge, and in the first column I read out a list of names. The second column described what had happened to them: who had been killed, whose property had been stolen, and who was now ill with dysentery or fever.

At the next village, Mirek again honked.

"Do you have a code?" I said.

He shook his head. "They recognize my vehicle."

The abbot stuffed each village's war report into his glove compartment. In the twenty-first century, this digital age, people here had been so isolated that this was how facts still needed to be relayed: by hand.

I said, "This is journalism."

Mirek laughed. "But no one has heard of me."

"You are humble."

Mirek used his position as the local abbot, a respected figure, known to the soldiers, to serve as an information relay.

In the distance, Bohong, the town of the massacre, appeared, protected by a lone soldier manning a barrier. The government still controlled this remote town. We had now passed beyond the rebel territory. The soldier sat on a wooden chair and drew up the barrier using a rope. Chickens clucked running around his feet.

Bohong's main road was dusty. Turning off it, we reached the church. Firmin got off the pickup's back, lifted the new door inside, and began to work. He measured the doorway with tape, hammered in new hinges on one side, and began to plane the door's edges.

Bohong's priest, Michel, stood with Mirek in the churchyard. Mirek presented him to me as *"Le père* Michel." The local priest had prepared a picnic lunch in a church gazebo. We ate chicken stew and served ourselves from a basket of avocados. I sliced open the fruit and ate it in spoonfuls.

"Will the rebels push the government back?" Michel said, in the impeccable French of someone who had studied at one of the country's prestigious religious schools.

Mirek said, "The rebels have not captured any big cities yet."

The rebels could seem like long-awaited saviors who would end the government's violence.

Michel said, "We can hope."

Rebel territory surrounded Bohong.

"I don't know if the rebels will behave morally," Mirek said.

Michel nodded. "Maybe they will want revenge."

Mirek said, "You desire but do not have; so you kill. James 4:2."

Michel nodded. "We should beware the things we want."

Michel led me through his church. Pockmarks had chipped away bits of its red brick walls. Michel pointed at a safe that had contained the tabernacle; soldiers had stolen the key, so he could not use it in his services. A priestly robe hung from a hook, a string of holes along one of its arms. The soldiers had seen its silhouette and blasted it with bullets. But Michel had been hiding in the library.

Firmin still worked at the door, chiseling a decorative pattern into its front bevels. Mirek watched him. He and Michel now needed to sit for some private church business, so Michel arranged for Rémy, a local doctor, to give me a tour of the killing site.

Rémy walked me out to the main road, and into Bohong's center.

"Are you a generalist or specialist?" I asked.

He said, "I am a nurse."

"Michel called you doctor."

"I was only appointed a doctor after the soldiers killed our real doctor."

We walked through a place that looked like a Roman ruin, of toppled bricks and pillars. People lived in charred houses whose roofless walls made geometric shapes against the sky. Some had blue United Nations tarpaulins pulled over them.

"I was forced to treat the soldiers as they killed us," he said.

"Show me your house."

As he led me into his neighborhood, Rémy said, "From the hospital, I watched Bohong burn. But I helped our enemy. They did not allow me to treat my wounded family members, neighbors, or friends."

In one house he showed me a human skull. In another he pointed to white fragments half buried in the mud. "A friend's spine," he said. The flesh had decomposed clean around the bone.

"I have sinned."

His house was half collapsed. "How many people?" I asked.

"Two hundred."

So the toll here had been even higher than in Gaga. And at last, Lewis had arrived to document it for the courts. Suleiman and he parked near the church. Lewis wanted to rush to the hospital. "Two hundred killed," I told him.

"I'll need time," he said.

But Mirek, still in a hurry, wanted to get home. "Don't stay long," he warned Lewis. "And don't wander off the main road. Get to the cathedral before dark."

"The pickup is still in good shape?" I asked Suleiman. "We've done a lot of kilometers."

He made a fist to show it was strong. Lewis had attached

a blue flag on a wooden stick to the pickup's chassis. It read
HUMAN RIGHTS WATCH in white letters. So it looked like
Suleiman drove an ambassador.

"We met a rebel in a village," I told Lewis. "They sent
a list of people who were killed. Mirek has it. They need
medicines."

Bohong's solitary guard, from his seat, raised the barrier
to let us out. I saluted him, my lips pursed. He looked startled. I laughed at him. I needed a little comedy, to play the
fool at his expense, after realizing how soldiers like him had
massacred Bohong's people.

Mirek and I stopped near Bouar, at a town called Vacap.
And now, when he honked, a dozen men appeared.

"Stay inside Bouar," one of them said.

"It's not safe out here."

I felt they wanted to intimidate us.

The government had recently attacked Vacap, claiming it had provided the rebels with special *fetish*, or magic,
which had helped the anti-balaka win its recent battles. So,
unable to locate the rebels' physical bases, the soldiers now
attacked their spiritual fortifications.

"Tell the government that Vacap is now *anti-anti-balaka*."

They repeated "anti-anti," and laughed.

"We are targeting the *aerodrome*."

"We have friends coming this way from Bohong,"
Mirek said, and he described Suleiman's pickup. "Take care
of them."

Once we were on the road again, Mirek said, "I have

a feeling that the rebels are now ready to conquer Bouar."
At the cathedral, I grew worried. But just as twilight fell,
I heard the familiar voices of Lewis and Thierry. I stepped
out of my room to greet them, feeling glad, as if I had found
old friends after a long time apart.

I slept in that morning.

Then I couldn't find the others—not in the corridors
or in the dining hall. Our pickup was gone from the parking lot. No one had informed me about their plans. In the
cathedral, Mirek had just given mass. The African Union
soldiers loitered in the courtyard.

The government would need to defend Bouar against
the anti-balaka. Outside the cathedral's gates, I hailed a
motorcycle. "Camp Leclerc," I said.

The moto-taxi driver made a joke. "Camp L'Éclair"—
Lightning Camp. And he smiled at his pun on the French
general's name.

We drove up a hill and past the garrison's signpost.
The military barracks were still painted in the French
flag's tricolors: red, white, and blue. Colonial-era exercise
apparatus—parallel bars and wooden hurdles—lay unused
in a field. Outside a low building that looked like an officer's quarters, a dozen soldiers huddled around a table
and ate lunch. I went over and asked for their commander.
They pointed me to a man sitting in a beach chair made of
purple-and-blue-striped cloth.

I stood on shiny 50 mm metal bullet casings lodged in the sand.

Bouar's Chadian commander had a heroic reputation. The United Nations officials had told me about Colonel Nassir. He was famous as a decorated former U.N. peace-keeping commander, an upright man who had warned civilians to escape Bouar before previous spates of killings.

I said, "These bullet casings look new."

Plucking a Bluetooth earpiece out of his ear, Colonel Nassir said, "The rebels attacked us two weeks ago."

"They reached all the way here? You don't have troops to stop them outside the city?"

He rolled his walkie-talkie from one hand to the other. "Do you know how to operate big guns?" he said.

He had confiscated heavy weapons in a shipping container, left behind at this garrison by South African soldiers. "They could win us the whole war, but no one knows how to use them," he said.

"Even the African Union soldiers at the cathedral?"

"They refused to help us."

"What about your commanders?"

"Bangui has not sent us reinforcements, weapons, or men."

The air was heavy with humidity. I looked up at the clouds.

I picked up, from beside my shoe, two bullet casings. Littered across the sand, the casings looked like cigarette butts. I put them in my pocket, as a souvenir for Nat. Two soldiers standing beside me began to argue: "*Tu vas me faire quoi?*"—You will do what to me? "*Toi t'es lieutenant comme moi*"—You're a lieutenant like me. "*Oui, oui*"—Yeah, yeah. "*Tu l'as pris*"—You took it. "*Il m'a piqué 1000 Francs*"—He stole my thousand francs (the equivalent of two U.S. dollars). Colonel Nassir's forces were running on empty.

I asked a soldier for a lift, and rode pillion on his motorcycle in the cool wind that had begun to blow across the highland.

The soldier and I became drenched in the rain, and by the time he dropped me off at the old cinema, in Bouar's center—near large boulders set up millennia before to shelter a small altar of stones, which was still intact—the equatorial afternoon downpour was over.

Fleur-de-lis flourishes decorated the walls, and the arched passageways that had once led into the main cinema hall were now bricked up. Central Africans had recolonized the cinema, using it as a kitchen where they prepared wood-smoked *capitaine*, a river fish highly valued for its almost boneless flesh.

Bouar's boulevard had almost become a pedestrian-only zone, because potholes had made driving on the asphalt impossible. Large trees ran down its center and provided those of us on foot with shade.

I visited a clothes stall whose vendor sold two kinds

of *pagnes*, cloth printed with traditional Central African patterns. There was the *pagne wax*, heavy and stiff, with resplendent colors; and the *pagne java*, of finer cloth but muted colors. I bought the *wax*, of a bright floral print, for a dress for Nat. And I wandered into a street corner wooden stall bearing the hand-painted sign SAH-YONG FILS. Inside the hexagonal stall, books were stacked up to its ceiling. I bought *Terre des Hommes*—which I knew by the English title, *Wind, Sand and Stars*—a memoir by Antoine de Saint-Exupéry that had provided him with the ideas for *Le Petit Prince*, one of Nat's favorite books.

Behind the cathedral, some anti-balaka fighters, prisoners of war, were held in a wooden enclosure, similar to a wood pen used for animals. The gate was secured by a single brass padlock. The rebels could easily break the padlock and leave, but they remained, looking nonchalant.

Nat called that evening.

She said, "Come home, *reviens*."

Worried, I asked if something had happened to Raphaëlle.

"I'm angry at women," she said. "We never tell each other how difficult children are. The pictures and stories are always of happy mothers."

I felt we were on the cusp of greater reporting. I had only begun to write my magazine piece. And it was a long way back: first to Bangui on one of those giant IVECO bush lorries, and then on a few flights back to Rwanda, from where I had a ticket to Canada for about a month later.

"I try to sleep when Raphaëlle sleeps," she said. "But I spend the night awake, and during the day she's crying and I feel I'm doing everything wrong."

Nat said her fears had come like a premonition. "Do you really need to go after that general at Gaga?"

My descriptions to her had perhaps been too vivid. "You can't even trust the government there," she said. "They've burned down churches." She was silent. "I don't want to lose you."

I said, "We were blocked from chasing General Hamad. But the soldiers are letting us pass through into other important places."

"Just trust me and come home. I helped when you wanted to go. Your daughter should grow up around her father."

I caught my breath. "It's my work, and it was also yours. Not that I need to do it forever."

"But we never had a child."

Before Raphaëlle's birth, Nat and I had discussed my journalism, and agreed that I should continue. We planned for Raphaëlle to travel with us to Africa and Asia. She had wanted as little as possible about our professions to change. So Nat's insistence was confusing.

I wondered if she had discerned something about the war that had escaped me, if she spoke from her own instincts as a war correspondent.

I said, "I'll go just a little further." *Un petit peu plus.*

"Listen to me, *écoute-moi*," she said. "No story is worth losing you."

Her talk was dramatic.

But that night I felt lonely, like when I had just arrived at boarding school in India, at the age of ten, my parents a thousand miles away in Dubai, and I had reached for comfort by hugging a toy my mother had sown herself and given me. During the day, I had kept the toy hidden under my pillow, ashamed to show it.

At breakfast, bathed by the light of the cathedral's stained-glass windows, I told Lewis and Thierry that Colonel Nassir likely didn't have enough men or equipment to defend Bouar.

The government, so brutal here in recent weeks, waited, exposed. The solar-powered bulbs flickered, then were steadily dim.

I said, "Nat wants me to return home."

But Thierry began to flip through his notebook. Lewis typed a message on his phone.

I would face Nat's anger, her *colère*, when I returned eventually.

I suddenly felt thrown into a void, bereft of her and my family, in this place I had known only recently and that felt the more unfamiliar for the rare accounts of it. Before leaving Shippagan, I had flipped through the *Historical Dictionary of the Central African Republic*, published in French in 1980, and *Voyage au Congo*, a travelogue published in 1927, in which André Gide investigated the unreported crimes of French colonial rule here. The more recent books I'd found were academic treatises aimed mostly at Central Africa researchers. That this country was hardly known to people abroad reminded me of how, almost a decade before, I had read an interview of a Polish journalist, in which he noted how few foreign writers, philosophers and poets—African or Western—ventured to such places, even in times of huge historical events, which then passed largely ignored, or written up as a few lines in a newspaper. Curious about places I was rarely presented with, and that I suspected were kept from me, I had made a journey, beginning out of university, first to Congo.

We needed to leave this war's peripheries. The anti-balaka clearly had the advantage in Bouar, and perhaps in other remote zones.

The anti-balaka operated a base, rumored to be their headquarters, north of Bangui. It had been shrouded in secrecy ever since they had created it. I suggested to Lewis and Thierry that we go there, as a way of now reporting on both sides of the war, and completing our work.

Lewis also needed to speak to the rebels, whom the government accused of several killings.

This secretive rebel base was called Point Kilometre 100, or PK100, because it was situated a hundred kilometers north of Bangui's main Roundabout of the Republic, from where all the country's distances were measured. Bangui's airport, at M'Poko, was near PK9; the capital's Muslim neighborhood was at PK5; and PK12 was the name of an important crossroads from which one traveled to the small cities of Damara or Boali.

The anti-balaka had so far been considered too disorganized to challenge the government.

Little was known about the anti-balaka's preparations, in large part because the area around PK100 was considered too dangerous to enter. Even the French peacekeepers, the country's best-trained and best-equipped military force, did not patrol it. Priests did not venture there. It was a black hole of information, and the war's center.

Thierry gave me the confidence to make this journey. His presence on our team had been pivotal. His official title was Human Rights Watch research assistant, but he was vastly more essential than this title suggested.

After Nat's precious introduction, which had led us to meet him in the Relais des Chasses and to Thierry agreeing to accompany us, he'd proven to be an impeccable reporter—double-checking our information, and rarely leading us down a false path, though contradictory rumors abounded. And as a Christian whose community was targeted by the government, he had almost never taken a side.

I said, "I'm learning by watching you work."

I took Thierry's agreement to go to PK100 as a sign that we would be relatively safe; in this way I remained true to Nat's initial inclinations.

———

In turning around, I moved toward home and family. Only, I took a circuitous route. I pursued the open ends in my reporting at the anti-balaka base at PK100. We also needed to pass by Bekadili, to investigate General Hamad's attack, from Gaga, on those four obscure towns that the boy, Jean Noël, had cited.

On our way out of Bouar, we stopped at the city's airstrip, from where passenger airplanes had once flown direct to Paris. This airstrip could now reinforce the anti-balaka's counterattack. Suleiman hesitated; he said Colonel Nassir had restricted access to the airport.

"It's because Nassir can't defend it," I said.

We made the detour.

Clouds cast a gloomy shadow over Bouar. And the grass around us grew taller until it dwarfed our truck. We only saw green. Suleiman slowed.

We arrived at the field. Bouar's red airstrip was made of laterite, a soil ubiquitous in Central Africa, rich in aluminum and iron oxides. Malleable when wet, it baked in the sun and became hard—making uncomfortable roads but solid airstrips. The Harmattan winds had already covered the airstrip in a layer of powder. A plane hadn't landed here in weeks. We shut our doors with bangs.

This ground felt holy.

I walked toward the airport's main building—small, like a two-bedroom apartment. A short man stepped out.

"Hello," I greeted him with a wave. "Are you in charge?"

He smiled. "My name is Seraphim."

I turned my finger at the premises. "Could we look?"

From his room he brought out a bag of bread and broke off a piece. It was too stale to chew, so I let it dissolve over my tongue. Seraphim was Bouar's meteorologist. "I help pilots," he said, "especially in bad weather."

"Which pilots?"

"Two months ago two Red Cross flights brought in medicines."

He pointed at the airport's radio tower, equipped with a satellite dish. And, inside his office, he showed me a radio set. He wore the headphones and said, "Oscar Kilo, okay!" into the microphone, laughing. An orange-striped wind sock fluttered near the runway. A plastic receptacle was half full of rainwater. It was his meteorological equipment. "*Voilà*," Seraphim said. "*C'est notre aeroport.*"—This is our airport.

"Are you safe alone?" I said.

"I am Bouar's only meteorologist, so I will be safe."

The rebels had already been here. "They knocked on my door at 5:00 a.m.," he said, smiling wryly, "before they attacked Camp L'Éclair." The "Lightning Camp" pun mocked the soldiers.

I had a sense of the war's quiet escalation. What had been hidden now emerged. Thinking about the future of the war put us on edge. And we had finished our stock of chocolate-coated biscuits. The plain LU variety had a drier and less satisfying taste.

———

All along our way we asked about General Hamad's attack. And near Bekadili, we were surprised that people spoke more freely than they had a week before. They told us Hamad had "probably committed a massacre."

Lewis whistled, and kept his lips in an O.

"If they're talking, it must have been bad."

But that was as much as we got from anyone: rumors. So, when we arrived, again, at Bekadili, we reminded its prefect that he had wanted to help us travel inside the jungle.

He adjusted his thick spectacles. "I guarantee you nothing," he said. "But since you have returned, I'll try." He summoned his town's drivers. Motorcycles could traverse the rugged, narrow jungle paths. From Bekadili we could get to two of the towns General Hamad had targeted: those called Camp Bangui and Dombourou.

I said, "We need three motorcycles, *trois motos*."

"But we don't know if soldiers are in the jungle," a driver said.

Another driver said, "We have to wait for someone to bring us news."

It was how news usually traveled after an attack: a survivor walked to the next town and, if they were not too frightened, told others what had happened.

I said, "We have to go find the survivors."

The drivers refused.

"They might be suffering," I said.

"We suffer too."

"More than those people in those villages?"

"Yes."

I said, "That's fine then, we won't go."

I waited, watching the drivers chatter among themselves. A driver said he was ready to take us; minutes later he said no, he was too afraid. I said aloud, to no one in particular, that if it grew too dangerous we would turn back before we reached those towns. Then a driver wearing a black singlet stepped forward.

He said his name was Guy.

I said, "Do you have two friends you can trust?"

He rallied a second driver. It took us another hour of cajoling, of yeses and nos, before we found the third. We filled their motorcycles' tanks with petrol.

Lewis said, holding up his closed fist as we left Bekadili, "*On est ensemble*"—We are together.

I rode on Guy's pillion. He wove between the trees at high speed. Soon after we left Bekadili, the forest grew dense, and our road became formless—the wild took over. We walked our bikes across a stream and up a hill; we drove over a plain of high elephant grass that cut into our faces, burning us.

Leading our convoy and stopping to search for the "*autoroute*"—a "highway" hidden in the grass—Guy spat on the ground from his physical exertions. He accelerated. I looked over his shoulder and could not see the road. "Is the road still there?" I yelled.

"Yes, it's here again."

"Are we all together? *On est tous ensemble?*"

Guy honked, and the other drivers exchanged honks; they were at some distance from us.

"Yes, we are."

"How many hours to Camp Bangui?"

"Two."

"But you said it would be one hour?"

"The road is long, no."

In the middle of the jungle, we came to a rebel village. "Peye," Guy announced. Two dozen men with rifles greeted us at the village entrance. They wore colored bracelets and test tubes filled with *fetish* magic powders on their heads. The rebel spies had tracked our arrival. They described our journey from weeks before, from Bangui to Gaga to Bekadili to Bossemptele to Bouar back to Bekadili to here. "The government has its own spies," they told us, "who might be waiting for you down the road."

So these rebels sent a fighter with us, as our guide, to look out for General Hamad's troops, still in these parts. Before leaving Peye, we took a group photograph, huddled together like a football team. The fighters adjusted their *fetish* on their bodies. We held our poses, as eight fighters had photos taken on each of their phones. We had documented our presence here before the most dangerous part of our drive. The rebel guide got on Thierry's bike, since they could communicate in Sango. We entered the zone of General Hamad's attack.

The guide refused to leave behind his homemade wooden rifle, and so made us look like rebel accomplices.

But we took the chance, hoping he knew this terrain and would help us evade the soldiers.

We turned corners and manioc fields came up on us. A bundle of clothes lay scattered on the road—I saw baby-sized shirts. A mother had perhaps fled this way with her children, and dropped the clothes.

The road forked. To our right lay Dombourou, where our rebel guide said soldiers were likely to be present. We turned left, toward Camp Bangui. Our engines rumbled.

A man lay, chest up, on the roadside. Half his head had been blown off by a gunshot, and white larvae wriggled through his face. Guy clicked his tongue. *"Un cadavre"*—a cadaver—"is a bad omen," he said. The corpse's fingers and toes were still whole, and had smooth skin.

Camp Bangui was burnt. Casseroles lay on the ground, still filled with food. Bits of singed black thatch hung onto houses. Flashlights, slippers, towels, and bicycles were flung from their places. And I could feel the life around me, the people who had stood here making food, drinking tea, and chatting with their neighbors not long ago. I smelled a corpse.

Lewis walked around like a headless chicken, distressed, his arms flailing.

Thierry stood in the center of Camp Bangui's empty marketplace and shouted out in Sango: "Come out! Don't be afraid. We are reporters and the government is gone." He shouted and shouted, calling out to survivors hiding around the town. And then, in the distance, we heard someone.

We heard her slippers slapping her heels. She had

emerged from the forest. She wore a red shirt and a black skirt, and she came running down the town's central avenue, examining our faces, as if stunned, and stopping for just a moment to shake my hand, and say, "Thank you, thank you."

She had heard Thierry, trusted him, and exposed herself. And she had survived. Others saw her and also stepped out of the forest. And in that moment, I felt our presence had overcome some portion of the fear instilled here by the soldiers. We had restored a little community and some trust in strangers like ourselves.

They ran toward our motorbikes, staring at their blackened houses. They asked, "Do people know what is happening to us?" It struck me how important it was, for them, that we had arrived here. They were hungry and injured, yet they didn't ask for food or medicines. They asked the same question that Holocaust survivors had put to those who liberated the Nazi concentration camps during World War II. Did others know what happened to them? If others knew, there was hope.

General Hamad's soldiers had doused their houses with petrol and set them alight, they said. They showed me burnt things that I did not know could burn that way—whole, like an animal grilled on a skewer: a motorcycle, a person, a school. The rebels had pushed back the soldiers, and were winning, they said, when General Hamad ordered the burning, out of desperation, signaling that the government would make their towns uninhabitable.

We shared our food and water with the survivors. And already, they rebuilt. Two men squatted beside a charred motorcycle and salvaged its parts.

We at last had proof of General Hamad's killing. More than a dozen people were still missing. But we ran out of time to document all the deaths in Camp Bangui. Guy said we should leave already, to avoid riding through the jungle at night. Our bike journey here had taken four hours instead of two, and now it was already 3:00 p.m.

I was exhausted by this point and could not sit properly on Guy's bike. I flopped from side to side, shifting my weight, and I made our motorcycle sway—until we spun, and fell together, and I had a bloody knee. Guy was mad at me. Himself fatigued, he struggled to balance our bike. My feet hit tree stumps on the roadside, cut to ankle height. They hit my shoes and bent my feet backward. The pain was excruciating. Guy told me to press my body into his so we made a single mass when our motorcycle jumped. We entered a wet patch, and our bike's wheels threw up the mud, and the back of my shirt was covered in red splatters. The tree stumps finally cracked open my shoes, so my unprotected feet hit the ground. At each impact on a stump or rock I winced.

I called out to Lewis. I needed to stop. He understood, and yelled our convoy to a halt. "We have a *caca d'urgence!*"— an urgent shit—he shouted, and pointed me to a clearing behind the trees. I was overpowered, at the mercy of my urges.

I got off my bike and trudged, sweating, into the forest

and did my job. Glistening insects scurried over the ground. And when I returned to our bikes, Guy was solemn. He saw that I had been affected by our journey, that my guts had given way, and he knew it could happen to anyone. When our convoy set off again, though I could not sit any better, he did not scold me.

Peye prepared for a revolution. Rebels penned in their livestock, carrying rifles slung over their backs, and they turned the cranks of their peanut grinders. Our guide told them what we had seen at Camp Bangui. They clicked their tongues. We were only five kilometers from Camp Bangui, but such was the risk in this war that until then, none of the rebels had ventured there to check in on that battle's survivors.

Our reports now riled them up. Like General Kalil, they declared, "We are the sons of the country, *les fils du pays.*"

They pointed at the test tubes of "medicine" pressed against their temples. "It protects us from the bullets."

"Our guns are good." They built long-barreled artisanal guns that shot metal pellets, mostly at small animals. So to kill a soldier they would need to shoot him with the pellets three or four times. Their ambition, to topple a government by defeating its well-armed military, seemed absurd.

"We will reclaim this land from our colonizers," the rebels said.

"We will move on Bangui."

"This war will need to get worse before we can be free."

Guy now drove by the moonlight. Our engines' roars

made a percussion with the croaks of the bullfrogs. I leaned on Guy's back, unable to take the journey anymore, unable to think about the city inverted at Gaga, of the maman holding up her bed, the woman in the red shirt running, and the feeling of shock in the burned Camp Bangui. The forest's leaves shone silver like blades. We passed an empty hut.

Children ran out of their homes as we burst onto Bekadili's streets. "Eyyyy!" they shouted. Guy drove to the marketplace and revved his engine to summon the town's residents, the prefect, the priest, and the imam. "General Hamad burned Camp Bangui," Guy started telling the crowd, "and killed many." It was another success on our journey. We, and these people, had won a moral victory over the government. We had recorded crimes that the government had not wanted to be known.

We had gotten a glimpse of what happened—and what remained hidden—across the country.

The story of what we saw passed from person to person. Each telling was defiant, rebellious. Warm beers were handed out. Bekadili's prefect, wearing his thick glasses, brought out two loudspeakers and set them up in the *majlis*, wired to car batteries. They blared a festive Congolese rumba.

Suleiman informed us that a government convoy had passed here. "The soldiers were following you," he said, "and they tried to confiscate my truck!"

"How come it's still here?" I said, looking at our white pickup parked on the roadside.

"I talked them out of it in Arabic," Suleiman said. "They wanted to know where you were, so I told them we will present our *ordre de mission* at the checkpoint, on our way to Bangui."

I lay on the ground, on the edge of the national highway. Trucks sped past my head. I absorbed Bekadili's euphoria and the thrill of our accomplishment. We had reached the scene of a war crime. Despite Hamad trying to block our passage, we had documented his killings, destruction of a town, and legal violations. I wrote in my notebook, drafting my magazine story, lying down, while Lewis, sitting beside me, typed out his report for Human Rights Watch.

"They'll publish it as breaking news," he said, "in a few days."

"General Hamad will know," I said, "and be angry."

But if anything happened to us, especially after we published a report, it would be obvious who was responsible. A reprisal against us would be reported internationally. This would likely dissuade him.

Guy lay down beside me. "Bekadili is sending help to Camp Bangui," he said. "Food, medicines, and materials to rebuild their houses." Our team had closed up one open end: General Hamad's attack.

Our success that day was a good omen, I felt, before we headed to the rebel headquarters at PK100.

I joined the villagers dancing in Bekadili's central marketplace. A woman pulled me to dance with her. She handed me a glass of palm wine, which I chugged, nodding to the rumba. I danced barefoot.

Early in the morning, the imam welcomed us into the *majlis*. He provided us with kettles of warm water and a piece of soap. I cleaned off viscous dirt stuck to my skin from our journey and then the dancing. We set up our beds—our mattresses beneath our strung-up mosquito nets. I listened to heavy vehicles driving by just a few meters from us, on National Highway 3.

Bekadili's families saw us off. The prefect gave us benediction in the morning, and the imam his blessings. Guy grabbed my shoulders. "Bekadili now fights together with the other towns," he said. "Muslims and Christians are united here." We made a greeting showing warmth between friends, bumping our heads.

I said, "I'll be in touch."

"I have your number," said Guy.

But our pickup's battery had died. Guy and the townspeople pushed us down the road. Our exhaust belched, and Suleiman's engine rumbled.

We drove in silence until the final checkpoint before entering Bangui's zone.

"Where are you coming from?" the soldier asked.

"Bekadili," Lewis answered.

We waited for him to order us to step out of our vehicle. We had prepared a speech protesting our arrest, claiming we needed to hurry back to Bangui for an urgent meeting with General Kalil. We were ready to taunt him, to make a fuss about General Kalil's anger at our lateness.

The commander stamped our *ordre de mission*, adding to our tally of colored checkpoint stamps. He said, "Okay." Suleiman accelerated up National Highway 1. His Chadian folk music rang out from our speakers.

I told Lewis, "That was a dangerous thing we did."

"General Hamad wouldn't have counted on it," he said.

"I don't know if I would have gone in on my own."

"I'd have gone in on my own," he said.

I raised my middle finger over my seat, so Lewis, sitting behind me, could see. And I said, "Human rights Rambo." The journey to Camp Bangui had brought us closer. I felt it was as though Lewis could not bear such closeness, and so he resorted to bravado.

Lewis needed to stop for a day in Bangui—to obtain comment from the government on the killings we had so far investigated. His updated report would keep bosses in New York busy, and free him up for our next excursion, to PK100.

"I should take down Niccola's phone number," I said, on hearing the name of the rebel headquarters. "Just in case." Lewis took down Nat's phone number in Shippagan.

I turned the radio's dial, switching from Suleiman's music to the news on the Ndeke Luka radio station, one of the country's most reliable, and funded by the United Nations. The newsreader spoke about "Opération Hibou"— Operation Owl—a government effort to round up rebels and hold them in an unmarked building behind the Air France office. "Soldiers are torturing rebels in there," Thierry said.

"Rebellion itself is illegal," Suleiman said. "They signed up to be killed."

We then heard a report of a car belonging to the Red Cross stolen in Bangui. Their property was supposed to be immune from the war, under international law. The thieves were still at large. President Djotodia had appeared at a church construction site calling for peace, in a show of religious solidarity. And a date had been fixed for a much-awaited national league football match. The station cut to Celine Dion singing " . . . spaceships between us." And the radio jockey, a woman with a husky voice, momentarily lowered the volume of the music to greet us. *"Bon appétit* to those who are eating. If you are resting, *bon repos."*

My soles felt cool and free on the truck's rubber floor mats. I needed to fix my tennis shoes. I wiggled my toes, rubbing off the sand they gathered when I stepped out and stretched at checkpoints.

BETRAYALS

ON BANGUI'S OUTSKIRTS, SOLDIERS SEARCHED OUR truck and made us step out. They were on high alert for two French mercenaries trafficking weapons to the rebels, according to Thierry. They waved us through. Our guesthouse in Bangui wasn't far. Soon, I could rest.

PK100, the rebel headquarters, lay on National Highway 4, which led north from Bangui all the way to the deserts of Chad. The rebel territory started, however, at PK76, seventy-six kilometers north of Bangui, near the city of Damara. The rebel leadership had entrenched itself in this wine-producing region, famous for its *peke*, a specialty made by fermenting the sap of raffia palm trees.

We called Bangui's officials as we drove through the capital. The spokesperson of the French peacekeeping contingent told us its soldiers had no immediate plans to enter PK100. We wanted their protection. "The rebels are too strong there," the spokesperson said. "They don't let anyone in."

I called Nat.

"We're doing interviews in Bangui," I said.

She asked with whom.

"The government. To finish up our reports."

"We're waiting."

I motivated myself by thinking that I would soon return home, to Canada, my journey's destination.

So I didn't tell Nat about our final movements across the country. My dependence on her, and my home, became private. I conjured up Nat's face for comfort, but knew I shouldn't call her for reassurance.

We rolled up our windows to keep out the city's smoke. In the middle of a main road, men burned rubber tires and waved guns at the soldiers' barricades. They goaded the soldiers to attack them. Stories of the small rebel victories in the countryside had been broadcast on the radio. The people had been stirred.

And the soldiers seemed on edge. At a checkpoint, a soldier took our *ordre de mission* and opened his shirt to show me his chest.

"The rebels can never kill me," he said.

His chest was pockmarked by scars: closed-up skin. Inside each mark, he said, lay one of the small hunting pellets that the rebels used as bullets. The rebels had shot him dozens of times, but he had survived.

At our church guesthouse, Lewis and I heard gunshots. I stepped out of my room. The shots suddenly stopped.

"Did you hear that?" I said, waiting at Lewis's window.

He said, "It was close by."

At the top of the hour, on the radio, we learned that those shots had been fired by soldiers, who had assassinated an opposition leader, a lawyer named Modeste Martineau Bria. In Bangui, he had become a figurehead for the anti-government protests.

The soldiers had shot Modeste dead in front of a crowd, in the middle of the day, at a marketplace near our guest-house, as the lawyer had stepped out of his vehicle. The government had made the killing a spectacle. And almost immediately, over the following hour, people swarmed the streets.

The two newborn kittens played in our guesthouse's yard. Suleiman had taken his truck for servicing at a garage, while Lewis had holed himself up in his room to update his dispatch for Human Rights Watch.

I missed Nat, and called home.

She said, "Raphaëlle cried all night, again."

It was her quiet reproach. My job in Shippagan, when our daughter had woken hungry each night, had been to carry her to Nat's bedroom for feeding. This had allowed Nat to rest. But now she slept with Raphaëlle and kept watch over her all night.

"When's the next flight out of Bangui?" she said.

I said, "I'll look up the date."

In my mind, I only needed to finish my reporting and tie up all the loose ends. But I could not explain this. Our conversations had become too closed. I hung up and decided not to call home until my arrival was imminent.

Thierry reported for work at the guesthouse. I ran into him in the yard. The church sisters had summoned a cobbler to repair my tennis shoes, broken open on the tree stumps during our jungle ride to Bekadili. I watched the cobbler sew his black stitches into the white shoes, and pull the string so the stitches were tight.

Lewis was about to call Human Rights Watch, and then Niccola. So Thierry was free.

"Do you want to find these protestors," I said, "who are angry about Bria's killing today?"

He suggested we check at a nearby roundabout, where the protestors had reportedly set up barricades. We stepped out of the guesthouse. The air seemed tense. I picked up distant gunfire.

A military truck passed us, a man kneeling in its back. Soldiers held his bound-up hands above his head.

Bangui's streets had become militarized. Pickups patrolled with soldiers sitting back-to-back, wearing open-toed leather sandals, as in Yaloke and Gaga.

On one of the streets running off the roundabout, I saw three flaming barrels. A crowd danced around them, chanting about the lawyer Bria. "The government should go," they chanted. They had slung guns over their bodies. Smoke rose out of those barrels in thick black clouds.

I moved closer, but Thierry held out his arm to block me.

"Look," he said. He had noticed something.

The cars driving down the boulevard stopped before the barrels and made U-turns. A man who walked past shouted at us, "Leave this place!" The smoke from the barrels piled on itself, fell under its own weight, and formed hypnotic swirls.

From one of the cars near the barrels a man stepped out, holding his briefcase high above his head to show he was not armed. He wore a white *kufi*, the traditional Muslim skullcap. The protestors charged at him. The man dove into his car but the protestors had grabbed his door—they pulled at his briefcase. The man fought to stay inside the moving car.

The police appeared, running in—their chief at the front, wearing a tall blue hat shaped like an inverted tin cup, like of the French *gendarmerie*. The policemen fired in the air. "Please leave," the police chief told me. "It will help us." His politeness was excessive. Thierry and I followed him, but slowly.

"Police! Police!" the protestors yelled, dancing behind the flames.

Soldiers now arrived: Chadian mercenaries from the president's elite guard. They surrounded the car and brandished guns above their heads as they escorted the man with the skullcap back to their truck. The protestors watched, sandwiched between the soldiers and the police.

"Please leave, and go peacefully," the police chief yelled on his megaphone.

The protestors took their guns into their hands. They opened fire. Bullets zinged above our heads.

I ran with Thierry, who ducked into an alley to our

right, and I followed him between the houses, running with a small crowd, leaning into a corner and then another as we turned out of the boulevard's line of sight.

These streets were empty. The other people had kept running and screaming. Before me stood a tall gate. I rattled its lock.

"Who is it?" someone said, from the gate's other side.

"Can we get shelter for a few minutes?" Thierry said.

They didn't respond.

The shooting had stopped, so Thierry and I returned to the boulevard. The soldiers and protestors had disappeared. But the unattended barrels were still on fire. A group of schoolgirls appeared on the street, walking in a line, laughing, wearing their pink school uniforms. They carried notebooks on their heads and held plastic lunch boxes. They made the boulevard feel calm.

Thierry and I walked back to our guesthouse, where Lewis typed on his laptop, his notes from Camp Bangui spread out before him.

We left the capital early, heading to the rebel headquarters, which would inform the second half of my magazine story. I had written out many scenes already, during our drives and on some nights.

Lewis had sent his reports to New York early in the morning. He seemed satisfied with our work. He said, "General Hamad is going to get a few phone calls." We needed to be careful.

Our truck's tuned-up engine made a steady high-pitch hum, a clean noise. Suleiman had added petrol to our barrel in Bangui. The roads leading up to Damara were heavy with traffic. Finally, we arrived at a large green sign that announced, "Damara, *Ville Séduisante*"—the Seductive City. It was decades-old marketing for tourists. The rebel leadership's territory stretched between Damara and Bouca, a small city farther north.

A pole barrier that swung on a pivot, manned by one soldier, blocked our passage. The land beyond this barrier appeared uninhabited. Its grass was fluorescent green. Inside, rebel leaders had hidden themselves from the French peacekeeper patrols as well as the government. The road made a thin red line between tall avocado and mango trees.

Next to the barrier was a school, now a government outpost. Shirtless soldiers in the yard pointed us to their commander, who had occupied a classroom and sat at a teacher's wooden desk.

"No one is allowed to meet the rebels," he told us.

We showed him our *ordre de mission*, but he frowned. "You need a special permission."

I said, "We want to find out what the rebels are planning."

The commander collected our passports, one by one, and checked their numbers against our *ordre de mission*. He flipped back and forth through our passports' pages, looking to see where we had traveled. He held our passports up to the light, as if they might be counterfeit.

All this took a while.

He then called his superior.

"If you go inside, you have to spy for us." This was the message from Bangui.

"We can't spy for anyone," I said. "Journalists can't take sides." The commander stared at us.

Lewis, Thierry, and I sat on cement steps outside his classroom. Thierry called the *directeur général* of the president's security, DG Issa, asking for permission. Lewis took notes documenting the soldiers' occupation of the school premises, which, under international law, as a site that children used, should remain free of soldiers and weapons. He said, "This is a war crime."

Two women were brought into the school and forced to kneel before the commander, outside his classroom, as if on trial. The commander paced the open cement hallway, hands behind his back. The women had come from the rebel territory.

"We want our motorcycles," one woman said.

"Soldiers confiscated our *motos* and use them in Damara." The commander said the women had to spy for him.

The women grimaced.

Lewis and I walked to Damara's market, normally the city's busiest area. But it was deserted. Dry manioc and raw red beans lay strewn over its plywood shelves. The market had been abandoned in a hurry. The emptiness: it was a sign that people had not felt safe.

"They sense the war coming," I told Lewis, as we stood in the empty market. I didn't want to spend the night in this ghost city.

To pass the afternoon, while we waited for word from DG Issa, I wrote out the soldiers' names for them in Arabic. I had learned the script as a child in Dubai. And I felt I performed magic for these illiterate soldiers. They delighted in copying out their own names, stroke by stroke, dot by dot, in their holy language. A soldier named Tamir handed me his rifle and promised to protect me.

"Ask your commander to let us through," I said. My throat had become parched in the heat. Finally, before sunset, when it was too late to travel very far, the commander allowed us to make a brief excursion into the rebel territory.

He said, "One of my men goes with you."

Lewis said, "We can show you what we will publish."

"I'm not your friend?" the commander said.

"Of course, of course, *si, si,*" I said.

"Then you can't be neutral."

As we left, his soldiers raised their rifles to make a salute, as if we were their emissaries into the rebel territory.

Our car made a crackling rumble on the dirt road. We turned a corner, and the road carried on, almost infinite. The jungle looked impenetrable on our either side. I sat up to look ahead. There was a sudden gushing. We were on high ground, and beneath us, under a bridge, ran a stream. A man bathing in it saw us, opened his eyes wide and hooted. He gathered his clothes and ran into the trees. More hoots sounded from the forest—not animals. A group of rebels stepped onto the road, their silhouettes a hundred meters ahead. Suleiman stopped and cut the engine.

A fighter walked up to our truck.

I said, "Where's your leader, *votre chef*?"

The rebels surrounded us and Suleiman drove at walking pace. The fighters' amulets, hanging on their waists, resembled the protective charms some cultures tied on their children. A fighter glanced at us, inside our pickup's cab, and smiled. They were deferential.

A land mine had been planted in the middle of the road. The rebels stood around the mine and directed Suleiman to drive around it. What we could see—the fighters, their weapons, and the position of this land mine—was valuable military intelligence. Already we were privy to the rebel fortifications and tactics.

We arrived at the first rebel outpost, a village whose houses had been burned, and then, over time, stripped of its thatch by wind and rain. Dozens of fighters arrived and vigorously shook my hand, as if I were a dignitary. "We're going to eradicate the Muslims," one of them announced.

"Eradicate how?" I said.

"No Muslims, no government, no problems."

I said, "Not all Muslims support this government."

"Don't worry, we have a solution. Muslims are foreigners."

It sounded like bravado, too extreme.

I said, "You can't eradicate them."

"Soon, no Muslims will live here."

Lewis was alarmed. "The Muslims are Central African citizens, like you."

"But they breed too quickly, like rodents."

"They are overrunning our Christian country."

The rebels sounded a little mad, as if, not knowing how to confront the government's killings, they had arrived at the most radical reaction.

Lewis shook his head. "Muslims have lived here for centuries."

"Because we allowed them to," a rebel said.

"They're a bunch of jokers," I said, about these men, in English. But my voice was high-pitched.

"I'm the chief here." The fighters stepped away and revealed a man wearing black devil horns on both his temples.

Zapramanza, the chief, said, "My men are telling the truth." He spoke without shame, easily, with certainty. "We have a saying," he said. "To harvest the corn, you have to kill the rats in the field."

In likening the Muslims to rodents he dehumanized them, so now his comrades only needed to follow the well-established logic of exterminating pests. He said, "It will soon be the season."

This plan had been crafted by the rebel leader who stayed at PK100, Zapramanza said. "Return tomorrow, and you can speak directly to the boss."

We recorded all of their plans and reasons. Their intent was clearly genocidal.

But Zapramanza politely shook each of our hands.

"Cigarette?" a rebel fighter pleaded with me. I opened our glove compartment and handed some out. The fighters lit them up in turns and exhaled with relief. Meanwhile,

Suleiman stepped out of the pickup, and held his phone high, clicking photos.

"Stop it, Suleiman!" I hissed from inside the pickup. "Not here!"

He said, "This is a dangerous place."

I made him delete his photos before we left the rebel territory.

I put my elbow outside my window and looked away from Suleiman.

And I noted our odometer reading: 92,489 kilometers. We had driven over one thousand kilometers since first leaving Bangui.

I put my head back inside the truck and listened to Thierry, Lewis, and Suleiman chatter about the rebels. They laughed at the fighters' joviality and ridiculous costumes. We were all nervous.

Then Thierry learned that our team had been prohibited from any further reporting. "Our *ordre de mission* has been canceled," he said. The government had finally taken action against us, after tracking us through Gaga, Camp Bangui, and to PK100. The minister for security and public order, Josué Binoua, ordered us to drive back to Bangui.

"We have to go straight to his office," Thierry said.

It took us three hours.

In Bangui's diplomatic neighborhood, Binoua stood in his office doorway, but stared over our heads.

"Who are these people," he said to the air. "And why do they disturb me?"

I said, "We need to go back."

Lewis's dispatches about General Hamad had reached Bangui, and the U.S. government had called Binoua to insist that the war crimes stop. Binoua looked above Lewis's head. "You have been *impoli.*" Impolite.

"With our hospitality, you traveled everywhere." He invalidated our *ordre de mission* and ordered us to get a new one stamped by three different departments. He was clever not to officially refuse us permission to travel, or deport us from the country. We could not complain, as yet. And the bureaucrats said our new paperwork would take weeks to process.

We called General Kalil. He said, "Who asked you to go and complain to the Americans."

Forging an *ordre de mission* was dangerous. And the roadblocks would not let us pass even a few kilometers out of Bangui without one. We walked through the diplomatic neighborhood. Some children played, pulling strings attached to toy wooden rocket launchers. The war had even infiltrated their games.

Thierry and Suleiman went home, and Lewis and I took a taxi back to our guesthouse, passing by Bangui's bars. We heard Chadian music. Trucks without license plates were parked haphazardly. Soldiers from the president's bodyguard unit stumbled out of the parties, women gripping their arms.

Perhaps the rebels would remain hidden until they launched their genocidal plan. We had no way to verify Zapramanza's claims. I still thought, and hoped, that they were making big talk.

We stopped at the stadium to purchase grilled capitaine at one of its night stalls, and then climbed the cement stairs to the stadium's highest floor. Sitting in two white plastic chairs, we stared into the open void above Bangui. A wind rose, sweeping dust and plastic bags through the corridors. There was thunder. A storm. The sky felt close, water pouring down onto the stadium's cement, and spraying on our faces.

Lewis said, "We needed this, man."

I looked over. His eyes were shut and he was smiling.

I enjoyed Bangui like a tourist. I was finally going home. I breathed in the cool air, standing on a hotel rooftop, feeling my smallness in the vast war.

Lewis and I spent the evening drinking cocktails at the five-star Ledger Plaza Hotel. Its rooftop bar gave a splendid view of La Colline, a hill to Bangui's east, enveloped in a moving mist. The loudspeakers played "Summertime." I hummed along.

Then Thierry arrived, and said, "I've gotten permission for us to leave Bangui. Binoua's order has been canceled."

He had persuaded DG Issa, the president's security director, that it was in the government's interest to allow us to confirm the rebels' plans. He said, "If more violence is on its way, the United Nations might send fresh peace-keepers." We still had plenty of fuel in our barrel. I called Zapramanza, but his phone was switched off. "You make sure we stay safe," I told Thierry.

I accompanied Lewis to the police headquarters. While we waited for the chief to sign our new *ordre de mission*, I stepped out and found Suleiman on the phone, pacing the street and gesticulating. He spoke about the rebels.

I rushed back and pulled Lewis out. We signaled for Suleiman to hang up. Suleiman strode up to me and stood against my chest. "What?"

"Who was that?"

"A friend."

"Talking about anti-balaka? You know we can't do that."

"I can't support my government?" he said. "Or protect my people?" He smirked. "Will you run in and save my wife and children when those anti-balaka reach Bangui?"

He was right.

But we couldn't keep him.

He had made us a rebel target by snitching on them. Lewis paid him the rest of his salary, and a couple of days extra. In his place, Lewis and I would likely have done as he had. He had little choice. Nor did we. Suleiman knew safety was our priority. We watched him get into his white pickup truck one last time, and drive off.

Lewis was despondent.

I said, "We're now safer."

Suleiman's spying might have helped us travel as deep as
we had inside the war, through all those checkpoints. But
we would never know. We had to prepare our departure.
Thierry spent the evening arranging for his fiancée to move
to a United Nations compound in Bangui, where peacekeepers would protect her.

Lewis and I took a yellow Nissan taxi to Bangui's
Muslim neighborhood, PK5, to find a new driver. The car
dealerships were all located in this open-air market, Bangui's largest. Near some caged live animals—sold as pets,
food, and as *fetish* magic—their shrill cries deafening, we
found a car dealer's office with green painted walls.

The dealer summoned one of his drivers and showed us
the 4x4 that we could rent.

The driver wore a cheap shirt, untucked. He was in his
midforties. "His name is Yusuf," the dealer said. "Do him a
favor and please give him some job."

Lewis said, "Are you willing to go to Damara, and then
PK100?"

Yusuf said, "I know Damara well."

Lewis described our mission. Yusuf stared at the ground.
To everything he nodded.

In the middle of all this, my mother called me, to ask
where I was.

I told her I was in Bangui, with Lewis. "Is everything
okay?"

"I just wanted to hear your voice," she said. "Keep me
informed as you travel."

That night, a Frenchwoman in her twenties visited us. Lewis and I met her in a small thatched-roof hut in the guesthouse's yard. Her name was Camille. She worked as a freelance photographer. "I heard you were traveling into the anti-balaka area," she said.

She had tried to get behind the rebel lines, and failed, and now planned to meet the rebels approaching Bouar.

Lewis said, "We might have a spare seat."

"But it's a new car and driver," I said. "And a new person is a responsibility."

We didn't know Camille.

We suggested staying in touch to see if a less risky opportunity arose. Six months later, Camille succeeded in meeting Bouar's rebels and was found dead in the back of a pickup truck.

I went to bed, leaving Lewis and Camille in the hut. And I had nearly fallen asleep when my phone rang.

It said UNKNOWN NUMBER.

"Hello?"

"We know you are meeting the anti-balaka."

I asked who it was.

"To meet the enemy is to take their side."

"We have the government's permission."

He hung up.

In the morning, we were carefree while loading our pickup, as if we felt it was our destiny to make this journey and nothing would go wrong. Lewis and Thierry did not seem concerned about my nocturnal call. "It's a prank," Thierry said.

I asked, "How do you know?"

He waved his hands. "It happens all the time."

A little over an hour later, we crossed once again into the fluorescent green landscape past Damara's pole barrier.

Zapramanza didn't stand up to greet us. He said, "You didn't come yesterday, as we had agreed. You didn't even call." He still wore his black singlet and devil horns on each of his temples. I showed him my phone, but he raised his palms at me. I wanted to prove how many times I had dialed his number, without success.

"We had to get a new *ordre de mission*," Lewis said.

"You met Minister Binoua?" Zapramanza asked. "He is the architect of the attack on PK100, coming this week. And today you have a different vehicle." He looked at Yusuf, screwing up his face. "Also a new driver." Zapramanza called up a guide named Delphin to lead us into the rebel territory's sanctum.

The rebel leader waved us ahead.

"*Balamo*, good morning," Delphin said, and got into our front seat. He wore a T-shirt and soccer shorts. I asked what his non-wartime job was. He said, "I'm a football player on the national team." He had played midfield in African competitions in Egypt and Morocco. He described the food markets in Cairo and Rabat.

"You're among the most talented footballers in the country," I said.

He said, "After the war finishes we can play."

"Speed up," he ordered Yusuf, and pointed ahead. "We haven't mined this part of the road." We obeyed his instructions—"right here, now left"—at forks. Yusuf drove off the road to circumvent booby traps. "The anti-balaka chief is actually near PK110," he said. So it was ten kilometers farther than we had thought.

The forest closed in on either side of the road. We drove through a tunnel of greenery. And I felt a strange sensation, like a premonition of death. This place stripped away my identities. I no longer felt I was a father, husband, or even a reporter. Nat and Raphaëlle seemed distant. Anyone whom I thought I could be was null: here, I was at the rebels' mercy, with few legal rights or protections. To pass into the rebel headquarters I had to diminish myself, to become nobody.

Following National Highway 4, which led northwest from Damara to Bouca, we reached a village called Mbourouba. Men were scattered over an open field here, arriving at this village from the bush. They carried their belongings in small bundles tied up in cloth. The anti-balaka had summoned the country's youth. Scores of young men had heeded the rebel call.

They'd had to walk in secret, hiding from soldiers and checkpoints.

"The government came here weeks ago," one villager

told us, "in fake Red Cross trucks." When Mbourouba's villagers had approached the trucks to request medicines and the doctors' advice, the soldiers had opened fire.

Lewis muttered, "Jesus, these people. Man!" We had stumbled on yet another war crime. This time, the government had masqueraded as a humanitarian organization.

Lewis could not let it pass undocumented, so we had to wait as he interviewed a dozen villagers, one by one, each conversation beginning with his lengthy preamble: "I am Lewis . . . I won't use your name . . ."

Mbourouba's headmaster meanwhile greeted me. "The soldiers pillaged our school's textbooks," he said, "for paper to roll up their cigarettes."

The headmaster was dressed in black, in a tattered jacket and shorts, and walked barefoot. He took us through the school. The blackboard showed the date war had broken out—23 March. The school was like a clock that had stopped in a bomb explosion. Classes had not reconvened since that day. The teachers had joined the rebellion.

"If we don't recapture Bangui," the headmaster said, "it can only be because God has turned his back on us. France will help us. France is our *papa*."

The village's pharmacist and administrative clerk had been drafted as rebel fighters, along with the headmaster. The headmaster showed us his rebel-issued homemade wooden rifle. He had received basic military training. These men, who had never used a gun, and were educated in pedagogy and accounting, took on the Central African army.

On our way to the pharmacy, I saw four young men—
"new recruits," the pharmacist told me—napping on a patch
of grass, their limbs draped over one another.

"The soldiers took everything," the pharmacist said.
Three white boxes of amoebiasis pills were stacked on his
empty shelves: his entire stock. Part of the pharmacy's roof
had fallen in, so I could see through it to the sky. He said,
"Do you have any injectable antibiotics?"

The rebels had run out.

"Simple diseases become life-threatening. We try to cure
people using medicinal roots from the forest. Many of us
have died." The desperate rebels fought in extreme poverty.

I said we were late for our meeting.

"Our commander is just a little further ahead."

Our vehicle was the only sign of movement in the landscape, the only noise. From the feeling of nothingness, in
this void, it came suddenly—I could not help it: a high-
pitch emotion, and a feeling of closeness with Nat. In this
desolation, she saved me.

I placed my hand on Lewis's shoulder. "*Ça va toi?*"—All
well?

"*Bien*," he said. "Good."

Thierry made a groaning.

"Ooooo."

He sounded unwell, but he was looking out the
windshield.

I felt a malaise.

A giant mango tree came up, and in front of it, a group of anti-balaka blocked us. More fighters emerged behind. Yusuf could not move in either direction, so he stopped. After a few seconds he cut our engine. A tall, broad-shouldered man in military camouflage yelled. I pushed my door open a crack. The guns all moved to aim at me. About three hundred guns pointed at me.

The tall man, the commander, ordered his men to encircle us.

"You lied!" he said. "You tricked us!"

Rattled, I yelled back, "Who do you think we are?"

Lewis held up our *ordre de mission*.

The commander said, "You're giving the government our military secrets."

Had Suleiman's spying been discovered? "Binoua has launched his attack," the commander added. The government, unbeknownst to us, was attacking PK100 on that day. The rebels believed the government had sent us out as scouts, under the guise of a humanitarian mission, to collect military intelligence.

"The government is following you, and the soldiers have already left Bangui," he said. "You stay on this road so when they get here they'll shoot you first."

Thierry, Lewis, and I looked at one another. We stood under the noontime sun, and I felt sweat roll down my chest, moistening my shirt. I glanced down at my cell phone, sliding it out of my pants pocket. We were out of range. There was no sign of the next village along National Highway 4. So I pulled out my notebook, kept looking up around me, and wrote down what I saw.

I nodded at Thierry. He gestured to the mango tree. He was right, we needed shade before anything. Lewis ducked into our 4x4 to collect his Human Rights Watch brochures.

"You can't leave," the commander told us, "until the government attacks us."

My head was hot.

It was completely rational, and therefore reasonable, for the commander to hold us, believing we would compromise him in the imminent battle. We had prepared this journey as well as we could have, sounding out Zapramanza a day before, conducting our own diligence, and obtaining the rebels' invitation. We had gotten unlucky.

I said, "Are you going after the Muslims?"

The commander unfolded our *ordre de mission*, carefully, so as not to tear it along its many creases. He read through our permissions, and inspected each of its red, orange, and black government stamps.

"Can we move?" I said.

He looked up.

"To the mango tree," I said. "We can talk in the shade."

He hesitated, and then pointed us to a long log placed as a seat beneath the tree. But Yusuf nudged me. "I'm going to the jeep," he said. He sat behind its steering wheel.

The commander and fighters watched him, but he stared straight ahead at the highway.

"No," I thought. Yusuf was at special risk, here, as a Muslim. The news about the battle had changed our calculus: we bore responsibility for exposing Yusuf to Christian hostility. The anti-balaka fighters inspected our 4x4's wheels and headlamps. The commander sat before us in a plastic chair.

"Are you going to target Muslim civilians?" I said, again. He said, "So, who are you?"

I looked up at our tree's canopy. The light filtered between its branches and silhouetted the leaves, their rippled edges and pointed tips. My premonition of death returned.

Again, I could not find the vision of Nat. The commander had taken away my sense of control, and of good fortune. I remembered the phone calls when Nat had worried for me. Thierry was still here, and our team remained together. The surrounding greenery, the giant mango tree, and the bright sky—they were unbearably beautiful. But now, writing this, I'm not sure if they were particularly beautiful, or if in that moment my mind only needed to find beauty.

A rebel to my left held his rifle at his hip, and pointed it at me. When he saw that I had noticed, he smiled. The fighters behind me drew up, closer. I heard their feet shuffle behind my back.

"Tell him to lower his rifle."

The commander looked over at the fighter.

"I can't talk while a gun is aimed at me," I said.

The commander gestured, and the rebel stared at me as he dropped his rifle to his feet.

I felt I had claimed a second small victory.

And Lewis started to work the commander. "Our team is helping your cause," he said. He opened a Human Rights Watch brochure and flipped through it. "Look at this report about a church burning," he said. "And this other report about massacres by soldiers. We have documented the government's crimes."

Thierry looked concerned.

The commander nodded at Lewis.

I said, "So we're just waiting for the battle to start?"

The commander turned to his fighters and ordered them to deploy as a perimeter at some distance around us. The log's bark felt rough on my buttocks. I began to shake my leg.

I heard a distant noise. Lewis and Thierry turned toward it. The drumbeat grew steadily louder. But it maintained its slow rhythm. The anti-balaka perhaps called their men into battle.

The commander said, "The U.S. used a children's vaccination program as a cover to attack Osama bin Laden."

"That was a crime," I said.

"But was anyone punished for it?" he asked. "The U.N. has sent French soldiers here to defend our murderous government, *notre gouvernement meurtrier.* But our people are punished."

I said, "Can I include those words in my magazine story? No one in France or at the U.N. has heard your perspective."

"No one can protect us except ourselves."

Lewis stood and spoke politely. "We have completed our reporting here, and will take our leave."

The commander smirked.

His walkie-talkie crackled. The commander spoke into it, and Thierry translated for us. "The soldiers are halfway to Damara."

The drumbeat continued. We ran out of time. "Where will we hide from the soldiers?" I asked Thierry. "In the trees?"

Lewis said, "We have very much enjoyed our conversation, and it's time for us to leave." The commander grumbled, his words unintelligible. Thierry stood and pressed Lewis down by his shoulders. Lewis resisted.

I yelled, "Lewis, sit the fuck down!"

He stared at me, mute. "You're going to get us killed, man. The commander will tell us when to leave."

Finally, Lewis sat on the log. He panicked, his eyes open wide. He had lost a sense of our position as hostages. We had traveled beyond the limits of what he knew and had previously negotiated. Now, like an upper-class Bostonian boy, he sat still, suppressing his terror.

I remembered when a thief had put a gun to my head eight years before, in Congo's capital, Kinshasa, and I had screamed. The thief had told me he'd shoot if I was not quiet. So now, remembering that thief, I stayed calm.

Time slowed, each moment dragged.

The commander's face twitched. Lewis's bravado, over weeks and months, had culminated in his paralysis. Thierry and I had to manage our way out. "*Ça va un peu bien?*" the commander teased Lewis, using a local expression that meant "It's not going so well?"

He said, "You won't leave this place because now I have proof of your lies." He had discovered that our 4x4's license plate did not match the one listed on our *ordre de mission*. We had fired Suleiman after processing our *ordre de mission*, which still listed his plate number.

"So whose vehicle are you driving?" the commander said. "Who sent you here?"

A ringing started in my head. "Shitshitshit."

"Your driver's name is not mentioned," he added.

I started to laugh. "It's just paperwork." The fighters moved side to side. The rebel to my left again raised his rifle to his hip, playing with me. These fighters were not trained to obey a chain of command. If even one fighter decided to shoot, the others would fire, and, in the chaos, kill our team.

I pointed out the rifle to the commander. But Lewis jumped in, telling him, "It's no problem."

"Back off," I told Lewis. "The guy's pointing the rifle at me, not you."

The anti-balaka fighter lowered his gun. Suddenly, he raised it. Then he lowered it again, and smiled at me. The commander said, "Your papers are erroneous, *erroné*."

"You're going to have us killed because of paperwork?" I laughed out loud at this absurdity. "Surely, you're more reasonable than the soldiers on our way here, who accepted our papers."

"Why do you show me a government *ordre de mission*," the commander said, "if you are independent of the government?"

It was an illogical argument, and I became frightened. I said, "We made a serious mistake. With your permission, we will return to Bangui and correct our papers."

The commander agreed. "Respect our laws," he said, "and correct your paperwork." In a surreal turn, he suggested that we could leave.

"Are you going after the Muslims?" I said.

"This government can't rule if there are no Muslims left to support them," he said. "We can't win in any other way." But Muslims constituted nearly 15 percent of the country's population, more than half a million people. And all at once, I saw the commander's vision come alive. "Muslim, Muslim," his fighters chanted, and turned to face Yusuf. One of them had recognized our driver from the PK5 Muslim market.

They circled our 4x4. Yusuf stared at the highway. The commander grew incensed: "You brought a Muslim here? So you are working for the government. What's his name?"

I called out. "Yusuf!"

He turned.

"Come and sit here." I patted the empty place next to me on the log.

He pushed open his door and, staring at the ground, refusing eye contact or any provocation, wove his path between the jeering anti-balaka fighters. They photographed him on their phones. "Muslim, Muslim!" They stood up to us and yelled in our faces.

Yusuf grabbed my little finger, like he was my son. And I remembered, at that moment, walking on the beach with Raphaëlle, her head on my neck. I knew why that image had arrived now. I was no longer sure if I would leave this place. I wanted to write a note to her and place it in my pocket, so someone might find it. But we had no time for such formalities.

The anti-balaka fighters entered our 4x4. It was a symbolic transgression: they had violated the only object here over which we had any authority, besides our own bodies. I had to stop them now. "Tell your men to step away," I told the commander.

A fighter held up a cell phone I had kept in our glove compartment. I shouted, "Put it back!" Another fighter wagged his finger at me. Yusuf knelt on the ground, holding my finger. He prostrated and sat up and mumbled his prayers. Then he looked up, at me, and said, *"Je suis prêt"*—I am ready. "If they want to take me, they can."

"Don't say that," I said, squeezing his finger. "No one's going to die."

My words lacked conviction. The fighters shuffled close

in behind me. I heard a murmur: *"Tuons-les"*—Kill them. I
felt they were about to shoot, that death was at last here. The
premonition had proved true. My back made a large target
for the anti-balaka. My spine felt the bullet about to come.

I looked up at the mango tree's green canopy. Everything here suddenly felt sacred. And I had the calm sense
that this, of all the places I had visited, was where I could
die. My body would be thrown into a ditch by the side of
this road. Who knew how long it would be before, perhaps,
a French peacekeeping patrol found us.

I needed to assert myself a last time.

I stood up from the log. I had little to lose. The commander was surprised, and, sensing my purpose, stood to
face me. *"Commandant,"* I said. "If anything happens to me,
or anyone here with me, it will be very bad for you." I repeated: *"Ça sera très grave pour vous."*

His eyes shifted, then stared straight at mine. I stared
back. "Lower your guns," he told his men. He waved his
hands downward. "Guns down!" But his fighters did not
obey and still pointed their rifles at us. They didn't trust us;
they had gone too far.

The commander said, "You can go, but your driver Yusuf
stays here." He needed to appease his men's restlessness after hours of working them up.

Lewis jumped to his feet. "We're all leaving together
or no one leaves." He had returned to his senses. I flashed
him a thumbs-up. I felt that we were on the cusp of getting out. "There are human rights laws governing this

war," Lewis told the commander. "Threatening a civilian is a violation."

"We take everything that's in your vehicle," the commander finally offered. His fighters agitated, looking for some victory.

I pointed to our 4x4.

The commander gave a signal and his fighters squeezed, many at a time, through our doorways, grabbing our mosquito nets, mattresses, flashlights, slippers, medicines, chocolates, and biscuits. Each compartment in our 4x4 was picked clean. The scene disquieted me. The anti-balaka, impoverished even in their headquarters, showed their desperation.

The commander turned his walkie-talkie's dial: a report came in. And he began to yell. Someone had spotted the soldiers' convoy at Damara. We bundled ourselves into our 4x4 and Yusuf fired up the engine.

The jungle opened up to us once again. Each thicket of trees welcomed us, I felt, every inch of land invited us to drive over it. I wanted to call Nat, to tell her we had escaped, but I couldn't, because I would have to first tell her that I had come here.

And we weren't yet out. The forest closed in on us. We drove through its dark passage. I felt I emerged through a perilous canal, through a terrible journey, into the world. The stark abandonment faded, and I regained a sense that I was somebody, with roots and community, a family and parents, that I came from somewhere. The trees shielded me from danger, while the highway led us out.

Near Mbourouba, we saw more men wearing city clothes make their way through the fields. And we spotted the government convoy, on the horizon, rapidly approach. We stopped on the roadside. The convoy hurtled past and charged toward PK100. One, two, three . . . seven trucks carrying soldiers, guns, rocket launchers, and bombs.

We stepped out of our 4x4 and turned toward the departing trucks. The people we had met that morning, in Mbourouba, would very shortly defend themselves against these soldiers, fighting with their homemade weapons. I remembered the headmaster, the boys lying on the grass, the pharmacist, the fighter who had pointed his rifle at me, the man bathing in the river, and the commander who had finally become scared, who had wasted so much of his precious time.

The government took on the anti-balaka at their center. And now the war allowed for no victory, in the greater sense of the word. The government and the rebels—no matter who won—would each perpetrate more killing. Violence had transcended both sides in this war. Each side claimed it represented the people. And each side claimed it fought for peace.

Delphin, our guide and a former football player, said I had surprised him. "They were ready to kill you," he said. "But you were laughing, relaxed." But when he said it, I rolled down my window and spat into the air. A few minutes later, we stopped for an omelet at a roadside food stall, and I got out of our 4x4 and spat and spat on the ground, between my feet. I made a puddle of frothing white spit.

I felt disgusted at myself, at this war, at nearly getting killed and having stood before people who had thought to kill me. It felt nauseating. Now I felt that anxiety. My words, which had gotten us out, had come from somewhere beyond my mind. They had arrived in my thoughts like a piece of luck.

Yusuf turned to me.

He said, "Could I please request permission to stop driving you?"

I said, "Sorry."

I had misjudged the risk to him. "We were careful," I said, explaining how we had gotten Zapramanza's permission a day before, as well as the government's permission to meet the anti-balaka. "No one told us the government would attack today."

"*Mauvaise chance*"—Bad luck, Yusuf said, after a pause. "But I'm glad I came. I saw and felt what is waiting for us Muslims. I need to get my family out to Cameroon."

At our church guesthouse, as Lewis and I got out of the vehicle, Lewis gave a cry and sprinted. He did it spontaneously. I chased him past the large gates into the churchyard. My backpack jumped high on my back. I laughed as I caught up to him, running as hard as I could. I felt I was with a childhood friend. We could both be boys. I was glad to be alive.

Killings or a massacre near PK100 seemed likely. Possibly many massacres, by the government or the anti-balaka, or both. We prepared to document them.

The radio news in Bangui did not mention the attack at PK100. Thierry said, "We are on the front lines like no one else in my country."

That evening, we bought ourselves a fresh stock of lollipops.

It had been four days since I had spoken to Nat. To earn myself time, I wrote her an e-mail. "I'm almost done, and will be home soon." Our journey was becoming riskier, and I knew I could not continue on such a trajectory much longer. This was where my family, and its security, had helped me arrive: at my limit.

My fear dissolved in knowing that I was loved.

Sleep returned me to lucidity. It was still dark when I woke, and while waiting for the others in the church parking lot, Thierry and I traced the easy constellations: Orion's Belt, the Big Dipper, the Little Dipper.

"People know more about the moon," Thierry said, "than of this war."

I told him the Big Dipper was called the *saptarishi* in Sanskrit, or "the seven sages" who looked down upon us. He said, "Oh."

We now circled PK100 to get to the battle's other side. We traveled north on National Highways 2 and 8, then west to Batangafo, and finally south to the city of Bouca, again on National Highway 4, but toward Bangui. We drove for two days.

The signboards announcing each city's moniker— Bangui as *la coquette* or "the shy," Damara as *la séduisante* or "the seductive," and Sibut as *la captivante* or "the captivating"—welcomed us like we were holidaymakers.

Hamida, our new driver, was a former soldier who accelerated and ran over the chickens that crossed our path. It was up to the people and animals to get out of his way. I looked behind and saw a chicken, on its back, moving its legs in the air erratically. Thierry said, "We have become the *Koto azo*, the important people." They were known for driving recklessly.

I told Hamida to slow down. "Our work is not so important."

Lewis taunted me from the backseat. "People are dying, and you're worried about the birds." But I felt we were callous, as if we claimed some power over death after escaping from the anti-balaka commander near PK100. We had forgotten how intimately we had feared being killed. It now showed in our arrogance toward these birds.

Hamida picked up a plastic bottle from near his feet and spilled tobacco over his palm and mine. He called it "*manga ti hon*," or "cigarette for the nose." He stuffed a fingertip of the tobacco up his nostril and inhaled sharply.

"Good?" I said.

He grinned.

After the high of the tobacco, I felt spent, and asked him for another fingerful.

"For what have we come all this way?" Thierry said, as we drove into the deserted city of Bouca.

The city woke us all.

It was Bouca's starkness, its grim dullness.

Soldiers had burned the land all around the city to smoke out the anti-balaka.

They fought a guerrilla battle here. The ground was black. Two pickup trucks transported soldiers on a patrol. We drove between the redbrick walls of roofless houses. Bombs exploded far away with a scattering noise amid the chatter of gunfire. The battle had spread from PK100 all the way here.

The military patrol stopped at Bouca's open church gates. Hamida parked to their right. A soldier wearing a red beret shouted at a huge crowd—thousands of people— gathered inside the church. "Rebels are hiding here. So tomorrow, in the morning, I will kill you all."

A nun wearing a blue tunic stepped out of the church residence, a whitewashed building at the compound's far end. "I'm sheltering three thousand people here whose homes are roofless."

The soldier replied, "They're lying. Order them to go home by eight in the morning. I'll kill anyone I find after that, including you."

So the soldier announced a massacre.

"We stay to report on this," Thierry said.

I didn't respond.

The soldiers left without speaking to us. Hamida progressed inch by inch through the crowd.

We parked before the whitewashed building, and climbed some steps up to the nun, who sat on a school bench in the church's main passageway. She held an old black Nokia cell phone, and dialed her vicar. She said, "I need help, they'll attack again in the morning."

We introduced ourselves.

"Angeline," she said. She was Italian. And she ministered in this dark city, of neighborhoods burned black, charcoal-hued earth, and the impenetrable surrounding jungle. Against this obscurity she made a pale figure, with ashen skin, white hair, and her bleached tunic. Her smile showed silver teeth. "If I force people to leave my church," she said, "the soldiers will hunt them down in the streets."

Either way, a killing appeared inevitable. "He is ruthless, Hassan," she said, of the soldier wearing the red beret who had threatened them.

"So we really stay?" I said.

It was early enough in the afternoon to leave Bouca for a safer place. But no one answered me. None of us wanted

to suggest leaving after Hassan had threatened to perpetrate perhaps this war's largest massacre. No one insisted on
staying at the church, but that's what we did. We had come
upon Hassan's crime by accident, as if it was our fate.

And so, once again, we found ourselves near death. This
time the sensation was less frightening. Nat, I felt, would
understand. I was sure of myself. And in a few days I would
be on my way home.

We asked Angeline for a room. She had already put aside
that morning's threats, and calmly, formally, welcomed us
into her church. "We have only one room available," she
said, looking at the ground.

She walked us down the church passageway and handed
us a key, and then showed us the communal showers. Our
room had been occupied by a church employee named Sarah
who was out of town. Her family photographs and note-
books decorated the room's wooden table. Besides us, and
the three thousand people taking shelter in the yard, the nun
also housed four doctors from the humanitarian organization
Médecins Sans Frontières (Doctors Without Borders).

These doctors confirmed Hassan's instability. They had
treated injured anti-balaka and government soldiers, without choosing a side.

Lewis and I called the French and U.S. embassies, the
country's most powerful foreign missions. Angeline warned
the Vatican about the massacre. Thierry called African embassies and local journalists and politicians. But the diplomats told us that people were killed each day in this country,

and they could not intervene. Thierry's journalist collective in Bangui spread word about the impending massacre, but got a similar response. The embassies and authorities would not stop the killing.

Then our phones went silent. All our phones, at once, couldn't catch the network. We could use Lewis's satellite phone to make calls, but we realized that the soldiers had switched off the cell phone towers as a war strategy, to isolate people, and prevent anyone from calling for help. Hassan acted on his threat. He prepared the morning's attack.

"Check our 4x4," I instructed Hamida. "The engine, water, tires. We might need to leave quickly, and our vehicle should be ready." I filled some plastic bottles with filtered water in the church's kitchen. I put a couple of bottles in our room, and stored the rest in our 4x4's boot.

I sat quietly on the bench in the church hallway until evening.

In the night, I walked through the yard.

Would the people stay? Bouca's prefect, wearing a heavy winter jacket, berated me in the yard for arriving only now, at the last minute. "Soldiers massacred 180 people three months before," he said. "No one came."

I didn't tell him that I hadn't heard about Bouca's killings until a few days before, and had not until then even considered coming here. The prefect wasn't aware that almost no one outside his city knew that his people suffered.

I helped Thierry lay two mattresses on the floor, then pull sheets over them, and draw covers over our pillows. Sarah's room had only two single beds.

Our beds looked neat.

I brushed my teeth in the communal toilets.

I spat out white foam streaked with red. My gums had begun to bleed because I ground my teeth at night from the stress.

I told Lewis, "We should try reasoning with the soldiers."

Instead of waiting for the soldiers to arrive here, we would meet them, and persuade them to change their plans.

Lewis checked with Angeline, who said no one she knew had approached Hassan since he made his threat. Two soldiers drove up to the open church gate and revved their motorcycles, provoking fear in the crowd, which started to murmur. Hamida drove us to Bouca's hilltop military base.

The soldiers wiped down their dismantled rifles. Hassan lay in a hammock, his pale brown irises resplendent, staring into the air. He seemed to be in a reverie, lost to the world. I offered the soldiers a pack of cigarettes—to create some complicity. Lewis watched me. I said, "It might make them kinder tomorrow."

We asked for the name of their commanding officer.

One soldier said he didn't know. Lewis tried guessing— but these soldiers, apparently, did not report to Noureddine Adam, the country's head of intelligence, or to General

Kalil, or to DG Issa, or even to the country's president. The soldier said, "We are a different group." If they were telling the truth, this made it harder to pressure them through their chain of command.

We drove back.

We waited with the people in the church.

Bouca's restaurants were shut. And we were about to cut up a few tomatoes, bananas, and mangoes for dinner, when Angeline invited us to dine with her and the doctors, in a room reserved for the nun's guests.

The Doctors Without Borders team leader was a Quebecois surgeon named Berthier. "Hassan is high on ketamine," he told me.

I asked what that was.

"A white crystal stimulant that makes him manic."

Berthier had tried to save Hassan's former commander, James, whom the rebels had shot in the liver some weeks before. At one point, James had looked up at Berthier, and said, "Doctor, I think I'm going to die." Berthier said, "When people have that premonition, death is very close." He had then only diminished James's pain. It was like a missionary's work.

The church staff had laid out a buffet of salad, boiled vegetables, pasta, and a fish. We ate behind a closed door, away from the gaze of the hungry people in the yard. Angeline said benediction. "The soldiers killed 180 the last time, and even the Pope could not stop them. Give us courage for tomorrow."

The church's gates creaked. Men crept out carrying their bags. But the majority of people here behaved as if Hassan had not come by that morning. They cooked their meals and rinsed their plates, which they stacked up neatly for use the next day.

On my post-dinner walk through the grounds, I met a mother who asked me for medicine. "My nine-month-old girl Mirabelle has a fever," she said. I gave her half a paracetamol tablet, and asked why she stayed.

"Soldiers have burned our homes and the bush," she said. "I have nowhere left to hide. They also burned my peanut crops." A gust blew into the camp. And she shook her head. "That noise of the leaves reminds me of hiding in the forest. The soldiers hunted us down like animals."

Vendors sold *beignets*—balls of fried dough—at food stalls. A man waiting in line in front of me said that a few weeks before, Hassan had beaten up Angeline. "He bruised her so badly that the church transported her to a hospital in Bangui."

Angeline had served as a human shield, putting herself between the soldiers and the people. In a conflict with few escapes, in which people retreated into the jungle, Angeline offered them refuge in this church. And this place had a natural power. People in distress looked to God.

To calm the children, the doctors perched a laptop on a low wall and played a science fiction movie. The children watched rapt, sitting cross-legged on the ground. The movie was about an extraterrestrial colony, another world, which made us forget the next morning. Angeline's figure paced the church's foyer. The camp became quiet at midnight. People slept in tents and under makeshift straw roofs.

A soft light shone on the garden and made beautiful silhouettes of the bushes and their leaves. It was the cabin light from our 4x4. Hamida sat at the steering wheel. I thought he tried to escape. But he was shirtless, and thumped his chest forward and back. I rapped on the window and startled him. He rolled down his window. Hip-hop music blared from the speakers.

"You're going to drain our battery," I said. I reached over to the radio and turned it off. The bottle of tobacco lay at his feet. I dragged him out of our 4x4 and confiscated its key.

"Go to bed," I said, and followed him to our room.

He made to lie on the floor.

I pointed him to the bed.

"And you?" he asked.

I said, "We need you sharp tomorrow."

I stood at the porch and listened to the crickets chirp.

My feet cracked the dried leaves. People snored. At one tent I heard a shuffling and then quiet, and saw inside the form of someone sitting up. I had disturbed them.

A shadowy figure walked in circles near where the movie had played. It was a Greek nurse from the Doctors Without

Borders team. He held a can of beer from the doctors' supplies. "Welcome," he said, looking relieved. He pulled up a chair and poured some beer into a second cup.

He was slim, and his face was covered in stubble. He said, looking nervous, "This is my first mission." He otherwise worked in a Greek hospital.

"I want to buy an apartment on a Greek island," I said. "As a place to write."

"The sea," he said, smiling.

We spoke of my dream of the apartment, as though it were imminent. It calmed us both.

"I found some good prices in Lakonia."

"Don't go there, they don't like people like us." He was gay.

"You should find a room with white stucco walls and a view of the Aegean," he said. "Skopelos is a good island." I wrote the name in my notebook, and over our final sips of beer, promised to buy a place there and invite him over. It was 2:00 a.m.

I didn't turn on the lights, so I couldn't tell who was asleep where. I lay on the floor.

There was a knocking.

I shone my flashlight at the door. Lewis stood still.

"I got their attention," he said.

"You did what?"

He had called the Human Rights Watch office in New York using his satellite phone and told them about the massacre at 8:00 a.m.

I said, "Let's talk in the hallway. The guys here are asleep."

Human Rights Watch had brought Bouca to the attention of the White House, the United Nations Secretary-General Ban Ki-moon, and the Élysée, the French president's office. The embassies had refused to intervene. But Human Rights Watch now had an employee here. Lewis's presence had suddenly made this church important.

I said, "How will they contact the soldiers here?"

"I don't know," he said.

"They wouldn't know the commanding officer's name."

"Let's sleep, man."

Lewis lay on the floor beside me. I couldn't shut my eyes.

He kept turning.

I consoled myself thinking of home.

Acadia came to me: its rugged cliffs on its beaches and at Miscou Island, where the sea was dark. I remembered lying in bed with Raphaëlle, our room smelling of her sweet breath. That night, the waiting emptied me.

I got up at around 6:00 a.m.

I had heard baritone voices in the yard, and the clangs of casseroles. A child cried. I dressed myself and stepped out into the morning chill. Women had started to smash corn in their pestles for lunch.

The church's bell tower was obscured by mist. I grabbed

a bottle of water from our 4x4's boot and chugged it. The doctors lined up against the whitewashed building, and Angeline waited in the garden, beside a statue of Virgin Mary.

The women pounded, as if counting the time. At 7:35 a.m. the soldiers began shooting at our compound. Bullets smashed into the church's walls. Still, the women pounded their pestles. The gunfire stopped. A lone shot rang out. Another. The people became restless and moved backward, toward Angeline, anticipating a mortar bomb.

Someone outside shouted at us, "Open the gate!" They banged on the metal.

A man in the churchyard shouted back. They started to converse.

"The soldiers want cigarettes!" the man yelled.

We waited inside our 4x4.

"Maybe it's time to leave," I said.

Lewis said we couldn't. "Not until the peacekeepers get here."

I said, "What peacekeepers?"

"Human Rights Watch stopped Hassan," he said. "The White House is arranging everything."

A doctor passed by our vehicle. I told him, "We're safe! The attack has been called off." He hurried away, and soon Angeline arrived. "You know what is happening?" she said.

"The White House called up Bangui," Lewis said. The

United States government had warned Hassan that Lewis should not be harmed under any circumstances. Since Lewis was located inside the church, Hassan could not attack.

A United Nations battalion had been ordered to move to this church from the nearby city of Batangafo. Once it arrived, we could leave Bouca, without the risk of triggering a massacre.

So Lewis's presence here had saved the three thousand people who waited in the churchyard. But he had achieved this by exposing the cruelty of our world. Three thousand Central African lives were worth less than one American life.

Angeline had watched helpless as nearly two hundred people were massacred three months before. "I thought nothing could be done for them," she said. "But for you?" Lewis had reopened her wounds. He had proved that the people here could be protected—the mechanisms and powers existed, but the world had to consider Central African lives as worth saving.

Lewis clenched his fist. "We did something good," he told Angeline. "We saved these people."

"It's true," I said, wanting to support Lewis in this awkward moment. Angeline and the doctors stared at him and left.

We waited in our 4x4 for word of the peacekeepers' arrival.

———

I called Nat, finally.

"I'll fly out in two days," I said.

"Where have you been?"

"I just finished my reporting."

She said, "Come." I had been run ragged by our journey. And speaking to Nat was a salve. I now had to unwind my way home: in a circular route through Sibut to Bangui, then in another spiral through Cameroon and Ethiopia to Rwanda, and finally in a third loop through Paris and Montreal back to Shippagan.

The church grounds were abuzz. "Lewis is a hero." People had heard how he had saved them with his satellite phone call at midnight. *"La haute technologie de l'Americain nous a sauvé!"* The American's high technology saved us!

Angeline stood at the church gate keeping watch. A soldier stood guard beside her. I asked if he worried about anti-balaka escaping the church grounds. He said, "The Muslims are fleeing Bouca."

It surprised me.

"The anti-balaka are about to attack."

Then Thierry received a report that the anti-balaka had won the battle near PK100. The anti-balaka now managed to threaten Hassan, all the way up in Bouca. Hamida drove me into the city center. The shops on the main boulevard, mostly bearing Muslim names, were barred with thick chains. A young woman wearing a black veil sat on a wooden bench before a large metal bowl. She lifted its lid to show me beignets inside. Behind her, on the boulevard, Muslim families climbed into a lorry.

"Aren't you leaving?" I said.

She raised her veil and said, "Do you want me?"

I shook my head. The way she saw me, it made me ashamed.

"My family can't pay for tickets," she said. "So I'm selling beignets."

I asked if the lorry tickets were expensive.

"The lorries have to pay men to fight off anti-balaka who try to kill our fleeing families. The anti-balaka men used to be our neighbors. Now they are exterminating us." So the anti-balaka commander executed his plan.

Muslim families dragged mattresses, cooking pots, and bicycle pumps along the boulevard's dirt. Bouca's imam, with a long red beard, coordinated the departures. He said, "A hundred and fifty Muslims are arriving in Bouca today, to defend the city and to protect the bodies of dead Muslims from mutilation."

A man on the boulevard grabbed a child and passed his finger across his throat. The child laughed.

A burned car without wheels squatted on the road. A four-pillared pavilion bore a sign for the French oil corporation: Station Total de Bouca. Through a house's doorway I saw the shrubs and trees of the jungle—the rear wall was destroyed, making the house's interior a part of the landscape.

———

We heard the peacekeepers had nearly arrived, so we drove out of Bouca. A few kilometers outside the city the convoy spotted us. A soldier waved from the hatch of an armored vehicle, so we stopped. Congolese soldiers jumped out and deployed in a perimeter. "*L'Americain*, the American," they said, pointing at Lewis. In their tone I heard awe. The Congolese commander reported our meeting into his walkie-talkie. "We have seen the American."

"Go straight to Bangui," he told us. "The road is still open, so rush."

On our way, I teased Lewis. "You know how to stop all the wars in the world? Put an American with a satellite phone in every village, and if anyone threatens to attack, the U.S. government will stop them."

Thierry snickered.

Lewis shooed me off.

"Yeah, yeah, guys, whatever. Let me be."

We emptied our 4x4 of all our equipment.

Hamida drove off to PK5.

Thierry would keep Lewis's camera as well as our mattresses, mosquito nets, and medicines safe at his house.

In my guesthouse room, I turned on the radio news. There was no mention of what had happened at Bouca, or of the rebel victory near PK100. Bangui was still under government control. The war was still caught in the silence, and we did not know what had happened a hundred kilometers away. Here, it could still seem as though the war did not exist.

Lewis walked past my open doorway. He said, "I can't travel like this again, man. I'm a father." We had forgotten who we were, that we were fathers. The war had swept us up in its powerful currents. I watched the kittens play in the dirt. When we told the sisters what we had witnessed, they decided to lock up the church and leave Bangui.

Lewis, Thierry, and I shared a meal of grilled capitaine at a riverside restaurant. As we sat on red and white plastic chairs, the vast Ubangi River stretched before us, the lone yellow lights of houses on the other bank, in Congo, turning on as it became night. A man wearing a fresh white singlet flipped our succulent fish using wooden tongs. Rumba played from his speaker.

I had set out on this journey secure in the love of my family, and trusting in my place at home, and now I returned to the beginning, to those origins. The airport in Bangui was crowded. The French peacekeepers kept it running. We waited at the gate, watching our small turboprop aircraft turn into position. And we ran into General Kalil.

"Cameroon," he replied, when we asked where he was headed.

"Us too," I said. It was a bad sign that the general fled. That battle near PK100 had turned the war.

"I wanted to bring peace," General Kalil said.

Just before takeoff, I inflated my traveling pillow. Lewis asked if I wanted to listen to his pop music.

He offered me his left earpiece.

SOLO

I stopped briefly in Kigali.

Lewis and Niccola invited me for dinner at their villa, and I took along a bottle of La Fin du Monde, or "The End of the World"—Quebecois beer. Lewis brought out his fine Scotch, and soon we were telling stories. When I mentioned Lewis's paralysis in front of the intransigent rebel commander near PK100, Niccola turned to him. "You never mentioned that."

It might have been Lewis's bravado.

I said, "It could be his trauma."

The journey had affected me. I had seen a pickup truck in Kigali transporting plastic pipes leaning on its back. But instead of the gray pipes I had seen rocket launchers, like those on the Central African government's convoys. I had looked at the pipes twice.

The next day I took a bus to the south. I'd kept a pet rooster while I lived in Kigali. On this stopover I discovered that he had died on the farm of a veterinarian friend who had served as his caretaker. So I traveled to the southern town of Nyamata to pay my respects to the buried rooster, and I wrote his name, Kazouri, on his burial hill, using white pebbles.

Lewis had been correct some days before when he'd said, on our way to Bouca, that I worried about birds.

My friend had conducted an autopsy on Kazouri, and she gave me her official veterinarian report of his death. "Kazouri died of loneliness, after you left," she said. "On our farm, we couldn't give him the same attention as you did."

In Montreal it snowed.

I waited on the platform and watched the Via Rail train crawl toward me.

I prepared my words for Nat, going over them. I wanted to tell her face-to-face how close I had felt to her along my journey. That the distance and the silence between us made me feel more intimate with her now that I returned. As I stepped into my railway carriage's warmth, I already felt her embrace.

I began the fourteen-hour journey east to Bathurst. It snowed the whole way. The trees, electricity poles, and people made silhouettes against the bright winter sky. I woke up at about 8:00 a.m., and glimpsed Nat standing on the Bathurst station platform. She looked relieved when I stepped out. I spotted no animosity in her expression. She said I should tell her everything: where I had been, what I had seen.

"But later," she said.

She was exhausted. When I got home, I unpacked my bags and started with my chores: the dishes, laundry, a supermarket run and a doctor's visit, after both Raphaëlle and I came down with the flu. My duties here, as a husband and father, were more private than my work and quietly comforting.

We prepared to leave Canada in a few months. Nat had a job at the United Nations in Rwanda, which they had kept open while she was on maternity leave. The job offered us diplomatic immunity, which would help my reporting on the dictatorship there, alongside Lewis.

A storm brewed near the Arctic Circle, not so far from Shippagan. Nat and I sheltered indoors, and followed the war on her television. For a short while, the war in the Central African Republic burst into the open, no longer hiding itself. The anti-balaka launched their massive counterattack from their hideouts.

The government should never have received the United Nation's support, but as the rebels rose, the government lost its foreign backers at that crucial moment. The U.N. passed a belated resolution to disarm the soldiers. Its diplomats seemed unaware of the rebels' strength. French peacekeepers forced the soldiers to lay down their arms, while promising they would keep the peace. But they didn't have enough troops to secure the country.

And without the soldiers, the country's Muslims became exposed. The rebels fanned out their army of an estimated hundred thousand fighters—from PK100 and other secret locations—against the government's few thousand soldiers.

More than a million Central Africans had fled their homes. One and a half million people suffered from acute hunger. Still, no one had counted the number of dead.

Bangui had been home to around 140,000 Muslims. In a few weeks, after the anti-balaka attack, only one thousand Muslims remained. The country's Muslim population fell by around 80 percent. Muslims were hacked down in their homes and in hiding. Many fled the country. The anti-balaka attacked mosques.

Foreign journalists flew into Bangui to document this carnage, which was broadcast live on TV and featured on the front pages of newspapers. The TV news broadcast images of men wearing skullcaps chased in the streets, swiped at with knives. The men arched their bodies, trying to escape. Spectators calmly observed them, their hands behind their backs, as if they watched children playing games.

Muslims' bodies were dismembered like they were toys. The war became an international spectacle. The overt attacks had a purpose: to publicly eliminate Islam from the country's national identity.

The U.N. sent in international investigators—people like Lewis—to document and assess the anti-balaka's crimes. These investigators declared the rebels' killings as "ethnic cleansing."

The investigators avoided using the term "genocide." The anti-balaka, they said, only tried to clear Muslims out of the country. They classified as exceptions the killings of Muslims fleeing the country. They didn't find evidence that the mostly Christian anti-balaka had planned to exterminate the Muslims.

International law classifies mass murders in varying degrees, based on such subtle differences in actions and intentions. A classification of "genocide" automatically renders an event and a people important to the world, to the United Nations Security Council, and to human history. Foreign nations are obliged to intervene and stop genocide, anywhere in the world, by sending in their armies if they have to.

So the assessment of "ethnic cleansing" spared the world from such responsibilities. Exactly twenty years before, in Rwanda, the United States and U.N. had avoided calling a genocide a genocide, and so they didn't send in the troops necessary to stop the killing.

The rebels' intent could be difficult to discern. They did not publish genocidal pamphlets or broadcast genocidal messages on the radio. They built no gas chambers. Yet they had been clear in their intent when I had spoken to them, even if their words seemed surreal, almost a joke.

And so, the necessary protection for Muslim civilians never arrived. It was clear that, through the genocides of the twentieth century and the pledges of "Never Again," the world had learned little. When these Muslims were killed, the world, as on so many occasions, instinctively turned away.

From the comfort of my bed in Shippagan, Nat lying

beside me, I followed the catastrophe. Food, medicine, and fuel quickly became unaffordable. The price of cooking oil rose from $1.50 per kilogram to $30.

The rebels killed with impunity, exacting their own justice upon those whom they perceived to be criminals, or children, who they believed might become criminals in the future. They carried out their own form of justice, based on the things they imagined.

The foreign journalists left Bangui after a week or so. The war faded from the news, and from the world's consciousness. The defeated Muslim government also retreated, into the northern countryside, where the rebellion had begun more than a year earlier. They declared a new Muslim nation and broke up the country.

Watching the television news, Nat said, "Did you travel to Bossangoa?"

I said I hadn't.

"Did you meet that official who's speaking now?"

I hadn't.

She tried to imagine me over there. And my refusals confused her. Where had I traveled? Whom had I met? The war broadcast on the television was separate from the one I had known.

"Tell me everything," she said.

At Christmas, we celebrated Raphaëlle's five-month birthday. My mother announced plans to visit Shippagan to perform the Indian rites customary after a daughter's birth—such as writing her name on a grain of rice.

My mother told me, "Find Raphaëlle an Indian name."

I looked up Sanskrit names online.

I picked up the magazine story I had drafted in the Central African Republic. How much of my journey was about the war, and how much about my marriage? Could I tell Nat how close I had felt to her, even while we did not speak, at PK100? Or was it cloying, and making myself too vulnerable, to say how she and home and family gave me the courage to explore the limits of the war?

I needed to pitch my magazine story to editors. How much would I tell readers?

A polar vortex hit Shippagan. Northern weather systems collided, and a low-pressure zone pulled in the Arctic Circle's cold. Temperatures fell to −40°, the point where the Fahrenheit and Celsius scales coincided, and it became unnecessary to specify the scale. My nasal mucus froze almost immediately when I stepped out of the house.

Nat, Raphaëlle, and I locked ourselves up indoors. I didn't mind this closeness after my time away.

We stayed indoors for four days. On the last evening, when our confinement started to feel suffocating, Nat said, "And what about your journey?" I felt there was nothing to hide from her now. I wanted to absolve myself of guilt for the distance between us, for continuing my journey after she had expressed her fears in Bouar.

So I told her everything, from the beginning, as if I

recited passages from my diary, or as if I was a storyteller
from an older time, before the Internet and telephones, nar-
rating a story that not many people had heard.

I was as honest and complete as I could be. I told her
about the spiral flight across Africa and my dislocating arrival
in Bangui, at the guesthouse with the bright lights. How at
Gaga we found the war's front line. How General Hamad
arrived with his platoon of young men and attacked the jungle towns of Dombourou and Camp Bangui. That the government blocked me from following him. How the children
played in the school, untouched by the war. That we drove
west to meet the rebels and document the massacres. That
the rebels threatened to capture Bouar's airport. I described
my journey to Bohong with the Polish abbot, Mirek, to in-
stall a new church door. The handwritten reports he collected
on our way from villages. Colonel Nassir and his men making a last stand at Bouar. The lonely meteorologist, Seraphim,
who shared his bread at Bouar's laterite airstrip. The motorcycle driver, Guy, who took us into Camp Bangui, the town
Hamad had burned. The woman wearing the red shirt who
ran out of the forest. How people asked, heartbreakingly, if
anyone knew what had happened to them. Our drive back at
night. The barrels burning in Bangui, at the protests over the
lawyer's assassination. How gunshots rang over our heads.
PK100, so dangerous that no one patrolled that territory.
How Minister Binoua tried to block us from traveling. How
Suleiman's spying for the government forced us to fire him.
And the rebel leader at PK100 who had his three hundred

men point guns at us. How he declared us government spies. How Yusuf held my finger and recited his last prayers, convinced he was going to be killed. How I convinced the leader to allow us to leave, just in time. The government convoy armed with rockets driving in to attack. How we reached the battle from its other side, at Bouca. That Hassan threatened to kill three thousand people sheltering in Angeline's church. How we stayed the night there. And how Lewis informed his office and stopped the massacre. The Congolese peacekeepers we met on our way out. Lewis, Thierry, and I spending that final day together in Bangui. That Thierry got his fiancée into a United Nations compound, where he would take shelter during the pogrom. And how Lewis and I flew back to Kigali, for dinner over La Fin du Monde, before I visited Kazouri's grave, and a few days later, caught a flight to Shippagan.

The telling drained me.

She said, "You're lucky."

"It sucked me in."

Raphaëlle began to cry.

I carried her to Nat, who became engrossed in feeding her. I waited, and when Raphaëlle pushed away Nat's breast, I returned her to the wooden crib in my bedroom.

A few days later, Nat and I disagreed about something, and during our argument, out of nowhere, she told me, "A man has responsibilities."

I asked what she was talking about.

"To your family."

"What's wrong suddenly?"

"You can make crazy journeys, while I've got to stay home."

I said she was still feeding Raphaëlle, otherwise she too would travel. But was I dismissive, I now wonder, as I write this?

"What kind of father risks his life?" she said.

"We've both worked in wars."

I felt defensive and did not want this fight. Perhaps Nat regretted the support she had shown me earlier, in connecting me with Thierry, in sending me off with so much love, and in encouraging me to pursue my work. She seemed angry—at me, and at herself.

Nat absorbed my experience of the war, perhaps for the first time. She held my face and kissed my forehead. "I'm glad you're home. That was your work, and one day Raphaëlle will be proud." And still, my journey intrigued and threatened her. "What did you feel at Gaga?" she asked. "And in PK100?"

I took her questions as signs of love. And over weeks of such conversations, I vividly seeded the war in Nat's mind. She imagined the scenes, places, and people, and the red roads that led us from place to place inside the war. "Do you have your *ordre de mission?*" she asked. I showed her a picture of it that I'd taken in Bangui, before we flew out.

I answered all of Nat's questions. I wanted her to know

me. It came from my desire to be loved. I had traveled in near obscurity, and now I showed myself to her, told her about that war and myself. She cared. "You knew too little," she said. "You drove in almost blind."

She ruminated on my words, obsessively, tiring herself. That night, when Raphaëlle bawled and I took her to Nat to feed, I found my wife awake, in the middle of the night.

"Can you stay?" she said, as Raphaëlle suckled. "I dreamt I lost you. Now I can't sleep."

It was as if she had returned to that day in Bouar, when she had feared I would be killed in the war. But now I stood in front of her. She lifted her hand toward me, and I touched it, one finger at a time, as if proving to her my presence. I got into bed, and put my arm over my family. The three of us slept together for the first time in weeks.

"I'll stay at home a while," I said. "The travel has caused too much worry."

I implanted myself at home, and in Nat's world in Shippagan.

In our basement library, I discovered a memoir by her great uncle, Gabriel Hudon, who had built bombs for the *Front de Libération du Québec* (FLQ), an armed Quebecois separatist movement. I outlined a story about his motivations for becoming a terrorist: his desperation, his fear of losing his identity and country.

I investigated Shippagan's mafias, which some years ago had burned down the town's fish-processing factories, but had never been held to account. The alleged mafia leader, a man named Anatole, walked around town a free man and lived in a mansion. "The story goes he was so powerful," Nat said, "that the police watched him and his friends drive in a convoy to the factories, burn them down, and drive back, and did nothing."

There were the Acadian stories from the Great Deportation of the eighteenth century, when English settlers in Canada sent thousands of French settlers into the Atlantic Ocean on ships in the winter. Many of the French froze to death. Some of those boats managed to turn around and steer themselves to the eastern coast of the American continent, including to Louisiana. The word *Cajun* is a corruption of "Acadian." Locals still demanded reparations for this old crime.

Nat guided me to interesting people who taught me about her community.

I came home from these interviews with stories that excited her. She felt me draw closer to her history and people. I wanted to write about Acadia, about French-speaking Canadians, and about Quebec's recent attempt to become its own nation.

It grew near the moment when Nat and I had planned to leave Shippagan for Rwanda. We had always planned to travel once Raphaëlle was a few months old. Our marriage had been constructed upon exploring the world together, in the exhilaration of making homes together, leaving them, and making new ones. But now Nat seemed to hint at staying in Shippagan.

"You should get a job," she said.

I said I already worked hard, every day. Again, I felt defensive.

"I mean work outside the house. Go to the office and return at dinnertime, like other men."

Our best chance at leaving then fell through.

The United Nations fired her while she was still on maternity leave, though technically it was illegal. "We lost our funding for your position," her boss wrote her from Kigali. By chance, Nat had received a second offer from the U.N. in Brussels, but that job started later, in the fall.

We waited out the winter.

The polar vortex pulled more storms into Shippagan.

Gales whistled outside our house. They shook our doors, which shifted on loose hinges. Snow blew across our house in horizontal streaks and piled high against our windows, rising up in white walls. They blocked all light.

After days of storms, I ventured out in the wind and, my face freezing, shoveled off the snow, so that we could see outside again. By the morning the snow had again piled up. And we began to live in this darkness. Nat reminisced about when we had first met, in Congo. She imagined my recent journey in ways that diverged from reality—by invoking her past. In the dark, and largely isolated, our imaginations gained power.

I grew uneasy about living in Shippagan's −40° winters.

I rebelled against Acadian life.

I asked, "Isn't this place uninhabitable without heating?"

This incensed Nat. The Acadians had returned to their homes after the Great Deportation, and to them their land had taken on a new meaning, as if they had recolonized it after exile. Their stories about the land resembled those in Israel. People often told me during interviews, "No one will ever throw us out again." The Acadians, descended from French settlers, had rooted themselves in the extreme cold, as had Nat, on this remote and infertile peninsula.

Before the Acadians arrived, First Nations Canadians had wisely spent their summers here, and left in the fall, before it got cold. Acadia reminded me of Dubai, whose 122° Fahrenheit summers made life there unnatural, possible only with air-conditioning. But Dubai possessed oil, so my father had settled there. Shippagan had a little timber and some peat moss. The cost of living here was exorbitant. Our monthly heating bill was about $500, half the average rent. The people of the Maritimes, as this region was known, cursed the winters but stayed.

I asked Nat, "Whose idea was it to live here year-round?"

Rebelling further, and sabotaging myself, I turned vegetarian. Though Shippagan was too cold to grow most vegetables. Its staple food was meat. The supermarkets didn't stock the variety of vegetables necessary to sustain my new diet.

Nat ate from my dishes at dinner. She relished the Indian spices. But I could not share in her dishes of chicken and pork. I found myself cooking larger portions, and becoming protective of my meals. I stared at her arm scooping into my eggplant or potato, and then watched as she bit into her pieces of meat.

Driving home, I saw schoolchildren cross the street, and I gripped my seat, as if Suleiman still drove me on the highway to Bouar. I had not been so affected by other wars. Nat's questioning had inadvertently caused me to relive my journey. It was embedded in my psyche. I had not anticipated the consequences of telling my story. It was as though she and I had invited my journey's panic into our home.

I bought a pair of cross-country skis, so I got out of the house. I had gained weight. I skied on a lonely trail through the woods and stopped to take in the silence of the white landscape.

I plowed ahead with my plan to escape a second frigid winter in Shippagan.

I told Nat, "Let's start a new adventure, move to Brussels or somewhere else."

She nodded. We looked up apartments together.

"How about Cambodia?" I asked one day.

She was excited. "When Raphaëlle turns one."

The months passed.

Nat said, "Raphaëlle is still so young."

She pushed back our departure date, then made excuses. It became apparent that she would not leave. She felt safe here. She had grown up on *rue Bellefeuille*. Her family lived within walking distance. And abroad, she would be forced to count on me. Without her saying it, I sensed she didn't trust me. So I stopped mentioning Cambodia.

Knowing I would not live here much longer, when summer came around, I took Raphaëlle out more often to the playground and pushed her on the swings. She gurgled with joy. At night, I took her from her crib and had her sleep on my chest, so she was comforted by my heartbeat.

Shippagan's community was bound by its shared history of suffering. Despite my Acadian daughter, I did not share their imperative for living here. Many Acadians had emigrated away from this remote peninsula. I obsessed about leaving. While searching for our exit, and hoping for a solution, I began to write my report.

I retreated into the basement, to my office with its orange carpet and no windows, where I read books that had belonged to Nat's father, and played his old vinyl on the gramophone. Sometimes I brought Raphaëlle downstairs to dance with me.

Fall arrived, and with it, the chilly winds that heralded

winter. I wrote my magazine piece at my desk, my note-books from the journey open before me. In writing, I tried to regain the internal peace that my home offered, the con-fidence that our family would again find cohesion, and the feeling in this cruel, confusing, and imperfect world, that I was loved. And that I loved Nat.

I fled from my estrangement with Nat in my writing, which bloomed. I described my journey from Gaga to Camp Bangui, on the motorcycle through the bush with Guy. The story was published by *Granta* magazine, and it later won a prize in London, which led to its second publication, in New York, as a short book.

Shippagan did not know me and could not understand me. A family at a restaurant asked Nat about her "African husband." A nurse I spoke with at a children's playground, while we pushed our daughters on the swings, asked if In-dia was in Africa.

"Not quite, but like Africa, it's far away," I said.

Nat and I saw a couple's counselor, in an attempt to regain trust. The counselor asked, "Why would you be a vegetarian? It's such a strange choice, living here." She also said, "I'm not surprised that you're unhappy. You should be flat on the ground, *par terre*, from everything you've lived through."

She offered an odd, rebuking empathy.

I had no friends in Acadia. My friends here were actu-ally Nat's friends. I called my best friend from childhood, in New York, and my mother, who lived in Dubai. But when those calls ended I returned to my bright orange–carpeted office, and my mind returned to its fire.

I found it harder to call this house my home. I began to refer to it simply as "the house."

Nat ate with Raphaëlle in the dining room. But she shut the door, and left me to prepare my own meals. I filled a kitchen cupboard with soup cans, and heated soup for each meal, throwing in sliced vegetables and shredded cheese for nutrition. I ate alone, in my office, listening to their footsteps.

Nat assigned me the assembly of Raphaëlle's new crib. It was an opportunity to perform my fatherhood. I spent the day joining the wood using screws and bolts. And I had nearly finished when I realized I had missed one screw. It possibly rendered the crib unstable. So I dismantled the whole thing, searching for where it fit.

What did it mean to be a father, a husband, and a man? Was it to be masculine, to protect my family, and be a reliable presence? Or could it be something more abstract, something neither Nat nor I knew, something that lay beyond our fears? Nat stopped asking about my journey. This frightened me more.

She now spoke about its consequences with finality. "You returned home in despair," she said. "And it grew." She said my despair had lasted months. "I don't know why." It might have been her distress about my journey, and nearly being killed, that made her now see so much despair in me.

I felt unloved.

She pointed out we had argued on the day I had returned. I said, "I remember a disagreement." But I couldn't recall its details. I might have started a fight because I had been too afraid to ask, straightforwardly, if she loved me. I sometimes did this.

"That could be," I told her.

Nat started to behave as though I were already gone from the house. I became something like a phantom, a ghost. She just ignored me, was indifferent. And I felt I had already left. I felt her frigidity when I entered her room in the evenings. She said, "What?" And turned back to her book. She found my physical presence and even the sight of me difficult to tolerate.

I had left home on my journey carrying a sense of my marriage's beauty. My work had felt pure. And my belief in my marriage, in my place at home, took me to my journey's logical limit. I wrote, to pass on what I thought needed to be passed on—what my family had inspired me to see, live, and learn. I had traveled with Nat and Raphaëlle as a family. My marriage felt no less true now.

"I'm lonely," I told her.

She said I could find my place in Shippagan.

My choices, decisions, how I lived and who I was: it had come to repulse her. As with so many marriages, there was no single reason for why I left. The end came after a period of estrangement and quiet torment, when neither of us felt loved. We lost our words. Something impassable had come up between us.

Nine months after I returned to Shippagan, I left home again. I felt I was no longer needed here, and that my presence was superfluous to Nat, now that she had returned to her community. On my penultimate evening with my family, I stepped out on the porch to look at the stars emerging.

I chose an Indian name for Raphaëlle. "Sandhya." That was my gift to her, an additional part of myself that I left behind. The name was Sanskrit, and meant "twilight." I had noticed that she was an evening child who came alive each day at dusk.

I made a second departure from Shippagan. At the time, I didn't imagine it would be definitive. I still hoped that Nat and I could fix our marriage, that distance could help.

My taxi pulled away. I looked out of the window at the fluttering kitchen curtains, and whispered some words to Nat. She was no longer beside me. But our marriage was eternal: it would remain so. We had only transformed from the people who had been married.

The taxi driver accelerated down the highway to Bathurst. I wanted to go somewhere remote, but I also felt the need to stay close. I wanted to turn back and feed Raphaëlle, bathe and change her. I felt lost.

The shrill peal of fear rang in my ears. My journey to the Central African Republic now seemed distant. My emotions were in a jumble. Now I felt despair, and now an inexplicable release from that despair. I could not locate my center within myself. I did not know where to move, bereft of my family. I needed some way out, some destination.

How would I live? For whom? These questions had lost their simple answers, and even their meaning. Would another anchor present itself, allowing me to moor myself and, from there, again live? The consequence of my love had been to find myself alone and to lose what I had loved. What did I pass on to Raphaëlle, if my choices had led me to such distress?

No longer a husband, and terrified that I could no longer perform my daily routines of fatherhood—that I needed to create my own ideas of fatherhood, and rituals by which to live—I watched the bay speed past, its waters like a blue mirror.

POSTSCRIPT

The Years After

MANY OF THE PEOPLE WE MET ON THIS JOURNEY died shortly afterward. Tony Montana, the child soldier in Gaga, was tortured by rebels before he was killed. Suleiman died of malaria, unable to procure basic medication during the conflict. Bekadili's prefect, who had worn thick spectacles and helped us convene the motorcycle drivers, was killed when the soldiers, defeated by the anti-balaka, pulled out of his region. Bekadili's imam, who welcomed us in the *majlis*, was then killed by the anti-balaka. A foundation was created to remember Camille, the French photojournalist.

A few acquaintances survived. Guy, the brave motorcycle driver who took us to Camp Bangui, somehow escaped the attacks on Bekadili. Mirek continued to carry aid to war-affected villages. Angeline allowed more people refuge in her church, protected by the Congolese peacekeepers. After our journey, Human Rights Watch hired Thierry full-time as a local researcher, providing him with a steady income. He saved up enough to marry his fiancée. Lewis was promoted as Human Rights Watch's Director for Central Africa.

I wandered across continents for two years after leaving Shippagan. I found work as a freelance journalist in Argentina, and as a teacher in the United Kingdom, at a school associated with a boarding school I had attended in India. I could have traveled farther away, but I stayed in Canada's orbit, not committing to a place while I carried hope that my marriage might rekindle. Nat and I met on a few occasions—in Washington, D.C., in Dubai, and India. Our separation was difficult, the conversations more and more tortuous, filled with the fear of loss. I filed for divorce, signing a heartbreaking settlement that guaranteed me nearly no time with Raphaëlle, because the law deemed that I was the parent who had left.

Raphaëlle and I had a gift of a natural closeness. As I did before my journey to the Central African Republic, after I left Shippagan I continued to tell her my stories. Recently, nine years old now, she began to tell me hers.

APPENDIX ONE

A Struggle for Freedom

THE CENTRAL AFRICAN REPUBLIC, SITUATED IN the heart of Africa, has for centuries served as an axis for migration and outside ambitions. In the seventeenth century, people moved to the present-day Central African Republic from the deserts to the north, in Chad and Sudan, and from the jungles to the west, in Cameroon. This area provided copious numbers of slaves to Egypt, Turkey, and down the Ubangi and Congo Rivers to the Americas.

In the eighteenth and nineteenth centuries Muslim sultanates dominated the area, extending their rule south from the Sudanese and Chadian region known as the Darfur. One of the most powerful of these sultanates was called the Dar al-Kuti, or the "door to the forest."

The fabled Sudanese warlord, Rabih az-Zubayr, captured Dar al-Kuti's capital and conquered the territory north of the Ubangi River in 1874. He co-opted local Banda tribesmen as his high officers while raiding the Banda and Nduka tribes for slaves. Rabih fought off the European nations—Britain, Belgium, Germany, and France—that competed to colonize Central Africa.

In 1900, France killed Rabih—beheading him for a trophy—and expanded its rule over what is now the Central African Republic, Chad, Gabon, and the Congo Republic. Before his defeat, Rabih's legendary resistance against the French created a myth of Islamic power here that endured in the minds of Muslims for generations, long after others had forgotten it.

The French-colonized areas together came to be known as French Equatorial Africa, with their colonial capital located at Brazzaville, in the present-day Congo Republic. French companies were granted "concessions": vast swaths of territory to govern, where they largely administered the law. Central African chiefs were ordered to supply people for French enslavement. The companies burned villages as retribution for workers' disobedience. In half a century of French governance, the region's population was reduced by approximately half. A Central African uprising against French forced labor, in the late 1920s, called the War of the Hoe Handle, was suppressed and its leaders executed.

France also inflicted whimsical terror. In 1903, to celebrate France's national holiday, Bastille Day, French officers blew up a Central African man by igniting a dynamite stick pressed into his anus.

To escape Saharan slave raiders, Africans had migrated to what is now the Central African Republic's Muslim-majority northeast—to the préfectures of

Bamingui-Bangoran and Vakaga—which the French authorities declared as "autonomous," too remote for central administration. The historical isolation of the northeast has contributed to its people's status as "foreigners," until today. Colonial authorities routinely referred to its people not as Central Africans, but as Chadian or Sudanese.

A degree of freedom was gained from the French in the mid-twentieth century: a Central African Catholic priest named Barthélemy Boganda—whose mother had collected rubber for a French company that beat her to death—rose as a national independence leader. In 1949, Boganda founded a party called the Movement for the Social Evolution of Black Africa. He was elected to the country's National Assembly, and used his platform to speak for African liberation, echoing the African independence leaders Nkrumah, Nyerere, and Kenyatta.

Boganda's vision was to create a "United States of Africa." The Central African Republic's generic name—more suited to a region than a country—alludes to its central position in such a continental union. Boganda believed African solidarity would counter interstate and European politicking. He rose to become his country's premier, but in 1959, a year before his country gained independence, he died in a suspicious plane crash that many link to French colonial authorities wary of losing their land and power.

France went on to dominate the Central African Republic's politics: orchestrating and supporting military coups and governing the country through proxy officials.

David Dacko served as the "independent" Central African Republic's first president, with French support. Corruption was rife in his administration. In 1965 he was ousted by his cousin and army chief, Jean-Bédel Bokassa—who fascinated Europeans by his desire to declare himself a great Frenchman. Bokassa boasted of his French citizenship and was crowned emperor in a Napoleonic ceremony financed by France. In 1979 he fell out of favor with the Élysée. French paratroopers flew David Dacko into Bangui and reinstated him as president. Dacko's army chief General André Kolingba seized power in 1981. France still governed the country by proxy, through a secret service officer who advised Kolingba.

When the Cold War ended in the early 1990s, France and the United States forced Kolingba to organize a free election. His challenger, Ange-Félix Patassé, won. Kolingba and Patassé deepened the country's north-south divide. They each nominated members of their communities into the country's most powerful and lucrative positions. Their forces attacked and burned rival villages. The army split by tribe. The country struggled to forge a national identity.

In 2003, Patassé's army chief, François Bozizé, gained the backing of France—and of Chad's President Idriss Déby, the regional kingmaker—and seized power. Déby provided Bozizé with mercenaries. Western nations sent Bozizé financial aid, calling him a new guarantor of stability. Bozizé tortured and murdered political opponents and rigged the 2011 presidential elections. Chadian soldiers called "liberators" protected him even as they plundered Bangui and burned northern towns. Resistance to Bozizé grew into a rebellion called the Seleka—"the alliance." Fearing a coup by rebels beyond its control, France sent soldiers to shore up Bozizé's power.

The Seleka, launched in 2012, was led by Michel Djotodia, a Soviet-educated theorist, and General Damane Zakaria, a military commander allied with Chad and Sudan. In 2013, its forces marched to Bangui and seized power. Seleka's victory led to the first Muslim government in this territory since Rabih az-Zubayr's Dar al-Kuti fell. As such, it represented a reversal of French colonial history.

Seleka's generals supplanted officials in Bozizé's predatory state structures, and continued to pillage the country. The fighters had been promised payment after Seleka's victory, but the government was bankrupt. So the fighters extracted their payment from the people.

An "anti-balaka" rebellion against the Seleka's government soon gathered widespread support. Nine months after the Seleka came to power, these rebels took over the country and "cleansed" Muslims from large sections of it.

Faustin-Archange Touadéra—Bozizé's former prime minister—was elected president in 2016. France then declared itself burdened by its former colony—though the world regarded it as responsible for the country's chaos due to its long history of interference. France walked away, claiming the Central African Republic's problems were not of its making. It pulled out two thousand soldiers.

Russia entered this void, training the Central African Republic's military, providing President Touadéra with body-guards and helping him reclaim territory occupied by rebels. Touadéra offered the Russians concessions to mine diamonds and gold. African minerals helped Russia circumvent Western sanctions after it invaded Ukraine in 2022.

Noureddine Adam, the Seleka's former head of intelligence, meanwhile, declared a new republic in the north of the country and called it Dar al-Kuti, the "door to the forest," after Rabih's nineteenth-century sultanate. The war had thus renewed an old dream of a Muslim nation. Adam tried to revive an Islamic history, and reverse the humiliation of colonization, and its attendant ideas of weakness. This new Dar al-Kuti, fragile and nascent, represented a return to Muslim greatness, to a time when Muslims ruled this land, built civilizations, and governed their own destinies.

France still held a strong hand on the Central African Republic through its control of the country's currency. Its treasury contained half of the country's foreign reserves, and served as a guarantor of the Central African franc in international markets. In a further attempt to escape its colonial past, in 2022, the Central African Republic made a bold move, becoming the world's second nation, after El Salvador, to adopt the cryptocurrency Bitcoin—which is backed by a mathematical algorithm and regulated by no central bank—as its legal tender.

APPENDIX TWO: Our *Ordre de Mission*

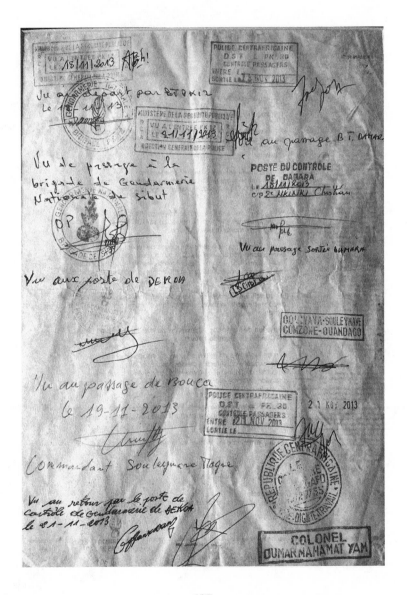

ACKNOWLEDGMENTS

Friends who accompanied me on this journey, in the Central African Republic, Cambodia, the United States, and other places. My publishers, Megha Majumdar and Kendall Storey, along with Laura Gonzalez, Laura Berry, Lena Moses-Schmitt, Megan Fishmann, Rachel Fershleiser, and the attentive team at Catapult. My previous publisher, Sonny Mehta, who passed away while I wrote this book. My agent, Sarah Chalfant, with Jin Auh, Jessica Bullock, and the excellent team at the Wylie Agency. The Berggruen Institute, the Rockefeller Foundation, the Skoll Foundation, and TED Fellows, for welcoming me into their communities.

ANJAN SUNDARAM is the award-winning author of *Bad News: Last Journalists in a Dictatorship* and *Stringer: A Reporter's Journey in the Congo*. He has reported from Central Africa for *The New York Times*, the Associated Press, *Granta*, *The Guardian*, *The Observer*, *Foreign Policy*, *Politico*, *Telegraph*, and *The Washington Post*. His books have been featured by Christiane Amanpour and Fareed Zakaria on CNN, Jon Stewart on *The Daily Show*, MSNBC's *Morning Joe*, and NPR's *All Things Considered*. Sundaram has also presented TV series for VICE News and Channel NewsAsia. His war correspondence won a Frontline Club Award in 2015 and a Reuters prize in 2006, and was short-listed for the Prix Bayeux in 2015. *Stringer* was a Royal African Society Book of the Year in 2014, and *Bad News* was an Amazon Book of the Year in 2016. Sundaram graduated from Yale University, where he studied mathematics, and holds a PhD in journalism from the University of East Anglia.